HONDURAS
in Pictures

VGS

Christine Zuchora-Walske

Twenty-First Century Books

Contents

Twenty-First Century Books
A division of Lerner Publishing Group, Inc.
241 First Avenue North
Minneapolis, MN 55401 U.S.A.

Website address: www.lernerbooks.com

web enhanced @ www.vgsbooks.com

Library of Congress Cataloging-in-Publication Data

Zuchora-Walske, Christine.
    Honduras in pictures / by Christine Zuchora-Walske.
      p. cm. — (Visual geography series)
    Summary: Text and pictures provide a close look at the land, people, history, government, and economy of this Central American nation.
    Includes bibliographical references and index.
    ISBN 978-1-57505-960-0 (lib. bdg. : alk. paper)
    1. Honduras—Juvenile literature. I. Title.
F1503.Z83 2010
972.83—dc22   2009004623

Manufactured in the United States of America
1 2 3 4 5 6 - BP - 15 14 13 12 11 10

INTRODUCTION

Honduras, a small nation in Central America, is a land of great beauty and diversity. Within its borders lie tropical beaches and islands, swampy lowlands, fertile river valleys, lush rain forests, and rugged mountains. Monkeys, wildcats, and brilliant birds inhabit the nation's woods. Crocodiles, otters, and many kinds of fish live in its waters.

Honduras's human landscape is as diverse as its natural one. The culture of Honduras reflects indigenous (native), European, and African influences.

For thousands of years, this land at the crossroads of the Americas has welcomed migrants from all over. Some people were nomadic hunters, gatherers, and herders. (Nomads move their home base according to the season.) Others were settled farmers and fishers. As the migrants mingled, they formed new bloodlines, languages, and cultures. Eventually dozens of distinct ethnic groups emerged.

Societies rose and fell, often battling each other for control. One of these, the Maya civilization, grew especially powerful. From about

A.D. 400 to 800, the Maya people controlled a large swath of Central America. Their empire stretched from southern Mexico to western Honduras. In Honduras they built Copán, one of their most important cities.

In the early 1500s, a new wave of people arrived—this time from Europe. The Spanish sought land, natural resources, and workers they could use to enrich their own empire. By then the Maya Empire had crumbled. Its people had blended into the tapestry of cultures that then made up Honduras.

Spanish explorers first subdued and then killed much of the indigenous population. Pirates often raided the colony. Spain and Great Britain fought over Honduras because of its gold, silver, and timber. Spain kept hold of the colony for more than three centuries.

Honduras became independent in 1821. But that event triggered 160 rocky years. During those years, Honduras suffered ongoing civil strife, foreign interference, and war with neighboring nations. During

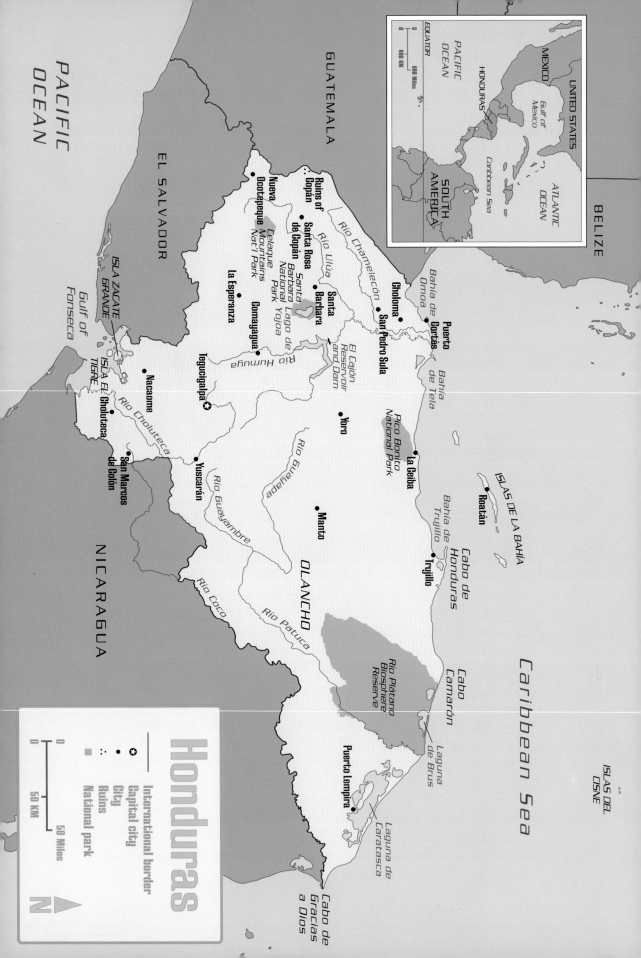

The capital city of Tegucigalpa suffered extensive damage during **Hurricane Mitch in October 1998.** The storm was one of the strongest and deadliest hurricanes ever recorded in the Atlantic Ocean.

the 1900s, a long series of harsh rulers and military coups (overthrows of government) plagued the nation. Military rule finally ended in 1981. In that year, open elections ushered in a lasting democratic legislature and a civilian (nonmilitary) presidency. In the late 1980s and early 1990s, Central American leaders halted all the civil wars raging in the region.

Although political and military threats had faded, Honduras still faced the forces of nature. Hurricane Mitch pummeled the country in October 1998. It killed thousands of Hondurans, severely damaged the land, and crippled the economy.

In the following decade, Honduras coped with its dependence on the U.S. economy. The September 11, 2001, terrorist attacks in the United States damaged both foreign trade and tourism. For years afterward, Honduras suffered from the U.S. economic slump.

In the twenty-first century, Honduras faces challenges. These include a large foreign debt; high rates of unemployment, poverty, and crime; and a wide gulf between rich and poor. But its seven million citizens take strength from the strides their country has made since 1981. The nation has free and fair elections, peaceful self-government, a diversified economy, and good international relations. It has put violence in the past and strives for a peaceful, prosperous future.

THE LAND

The word *honduras* means "depths" in Spanish. European explorer Christopher Columbus introduced this name in 1502, when he sheltered on the Honduran coast during a terrible storm. In his diary, Columbus expressed gratitude for his escape from the "treacherous depths" of the Caribbean Sea. Although this name refers to the sea, Honduras is also an apt name for the nation's land. Rugged mountains and thick vegetation cover most of the country. Farms and villages nestle in isolated valleys among large tracts of wilderness.

Honduras is a small country in Central America. Its shape resembles an upside-down triangle. The top side of the triangle is a northern coast on the Caribbean Sea. Another side of the triangle is Honduras's southeastern border with Nicaragua. The southern point of the triangle is a short shoreline on the Gulf of Fonseca, an inlet of the Pacific Ocean. The third side of the triangle is Honduras's border with El Salvador on the southwest and Guatemala on the northwest.

Honduras stretches about 197 miles (317 kilometers) at its widest point from north to south. Its widest point from east to west spans about 412 miles (663 km). Honduras covers an area of 43,278 square miles (112,090 square km). It's about the same size as the U.S. state of Virginia.

▷ Topography

Twenty-five million years ago, open sea separated North and South America. About that time, two large plates of Earth's crust under the ocean began inching toward each other. As they collided, the western plate plowed under the eastern one. The collision gave birth to a chain of underwater volcanoes.

As the plates continued colliding, the volcanoes kept erupting, eventually forming islands. By three million years ago, Central America had become a continuous landmass. The geological activity (Earth movements) that formed Central America has continued ever since. As a result, much of the region is mountainous.

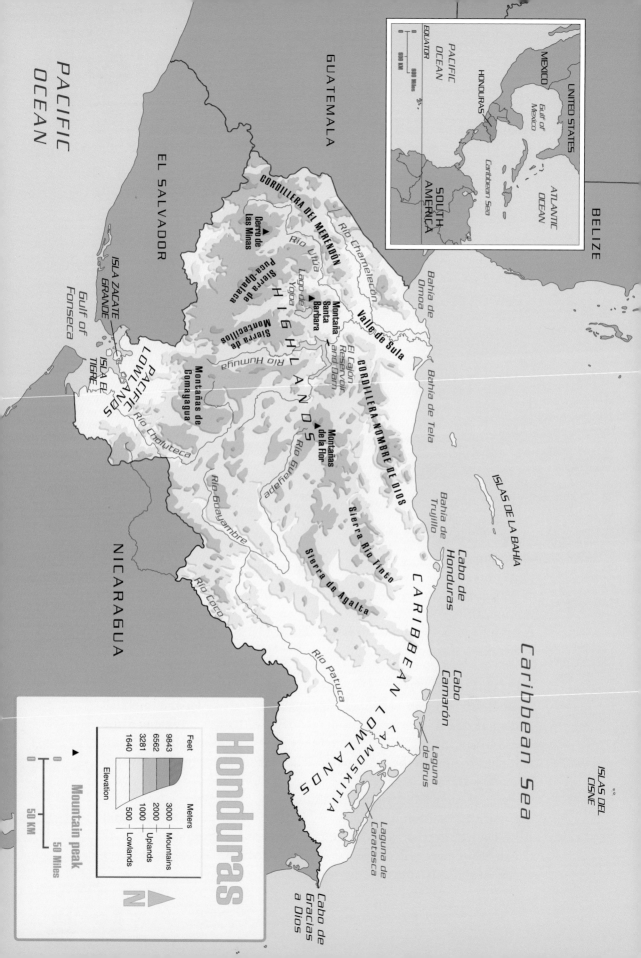

Honduras is the most mountainous Central American country. About 80 percent of Honduras's terrain consists of mountains, plateaus (elevated plains), high valleys, and rolling hills. These highlands form more than a dozen distinct ranges.

The long Cordillera del Merendón follows Honduras's western border. East of this range, Celaque Mountains National Park contains Honduras's highest peak, Cerro de las Minas. This mountain rises 9,349 feet (2,850 meters) above sea level. Farther east lie the Sierra de Puca-Opalaca and the Sierra de Montecillos. North of these ranges, Santa Barbara National Park contains Honduras's second-highest mountain. Montaña Santa Barbara climbs to 9,003 feet (2,744 m).

A deep rift runs through the highlands from the northern city of San Pedro Sula to El Salvador's eastern edge. East of this trough rise the Montañas de Comayagua and the Montañas de la Flor. The Cordillera Nombre de Dios range parallels the Caribbean coast near the city of La Ceiba. To the southeast lie eight smaller ranges, including the Sierra Río Tinto and the Sierra de Agalta.

Although Honduras is mostly mountainous, it also contains two distinct lowlands. A smaller lowland runs along Honduras's southern coast. These Pacific Lowlands make up about 2 percent of the nation's terrain. A larger lowland runs along the northern coast. These Caribbean Lowlands make up about 18 percent of the nation's terrain. At its western end, the lowlands extend many miles inland along the river valley of Río Ulúa. The lowlands' central section, from La Ceiba to the city of Trujillo, is very narrow. East of Trujillo, the lowlands widen again. At the eastern end, the region extends all the way south to the Nicaraguan border. Hondurans call this region La Moskitia.

Many islands belong to Honduras. The tiny Islas del Cisne lie about 95 miles (153 km) off the northern coast. They are uninhabited except for a small navy base. The larger Islas de la Bahía lie about 30 miles (48 km) off the northern coast. These islands are famous for their sandy beaches, clear water, and coral reefs. Honduras also has several islands off its southern coast. The two largest, Isla Zacate Grande and Isla El Tigre, are inactive volcanoes.

SPANISH PLACE-NAMES

The names of Honduras's mountains, rivers, and other geographical features use the following Spanish terms:

bahía: bay
cabo: cape
cerro: hill
cordillera: mountain range
isla: island
lago: lake
laguna: lagoon
montaña: mountain
puerto: port
río: river
sierra: mountain range
valle: valley

◐ Rivers and Lakes

Honduras is home to many rivers, large and small. They wind among the highlands and across the lowlands, eventually emptying into both oceans. The watershed (dividing ridge) between Atlantic- and Pacific-bound rivers lies in southern Honduras. As a result, more of the country's rivers flow northward.

Water levels change dramatically throughout the year. During the rainy season the rivers swell, often flooding the surrounding country-side. In the dry season water levels drop. Some streams run dry.

Honduras is home to the 466-mile (750 km) Río Coco, Central America's longest river. It originates near San Marcos de Colón in southwestern Honduras, flows eastward through Nicaragua, then forms about half the border between Honduras and Nicaragua. It emp-ties into the Caribbean Sea.

Río Patuca, Central America's second-longest river, also flows through Honduras. It forms where the Río Guayape and Río Guayambre meet. It runs for a total of 368 miles (592 km) through the central highlands and eastern lowlands. Río Patuca crosses several rapids and waterfalls before emptying into the Caribbean. This river serves as the main means of transportation and communications for La Moskitia.

Honduras's third-longest—but most important—river is Río Ulúa. Along with its many tributaries (feeder streams), the Ulúa flows northward for 222 miles (358 km) through western Honduras. It drains the Valle de Sula, Honduras's most densely populated, heavily farmed, and highly developed region. After passing San Pedro Sula,

The **Rio Copán** in Honduras runs near the ruins at Copán. Mountains surround the river valley.

the nation's economic capital, Río Ulúa empties into the Caribbean at Puerto Cortés, the country's largest port.

Southern Honduras contains several rivers bound for the Gulf of Fonseca. Only one is large. Río Choluteca rises in the highlands west of Tegucigalpa, the capital city. It arcs east through the capital and then south, flowing 217 miles (349 km) before emptying into the sea.

Honduras has one large natural lake. Lago de Yojoa lies in west-central Honduras. It measures about 14 miles (22 km) long and 9 miles (14 km) wide. Volcanic action formed the lake. Just east of Lago de Yojoa lies a large artificial lake. This lake is a reservoir formed by the El Cajón dam on Río Humuya.

About a dozen brackish lagoons line the Caribbean coast of Honduras. (Brackish water forms when freshwater and seawater mix.) The largest is Laguna de Caratasca, 31 miles (50 km) long and 7 miles (11 km) wide.

In 1998 Hurricane Mitch killed nearly seven thousand Hondurans. Flooding along Río Choluteca was a major culprit. The river washed out whole neighborhoods in Tegucigalpa. It swelled to six times its normal size in the city of Choluteca, causing even more damage there, then destroyed entire villages as it continued to the sea.

◉ Climate

Honduras lies near the equator, so its climate is warm overall. Weather varies more by time of day and location than by time of year. Altitude and slope are key factors. Temperature drops as altitude climbs. And because the wind usually blows from the north and west, slopes facing in those directions get more rain than those facing south and east.

The Caribbean Lowlands climate is consistently hot and humid. Daytime highs average from 82°F (28°C) to 90°F (32°C) year-round. In December or January, a large cold front from the north may bring several days of strong northwesterly winds and slightly cooler temperatures. Rain falls reliably all year. In La Moskitia, average annual rainfall is 94 inches (240 centimeters). Near San Pedro Sula, a bit less rain falls from November to April. But average annual rainfall there still exceeds 80 inches (203 cm).

The Pacific Lowlands climate varies from hot and dry to hot and wet. The dry season occurs from November to April. The rainy season runs from May to October. April brings the warmest temperatures, and the rainy season is slightly cooler. Daytime highs average from 82°F (28°C) to 90°F (32°C).

Honduras's highland climate is moderate. Extreme temperatures and rainfall are rare, but weather varies from place to place. Tegucigalpa lies in a sheltered valley at 3,281 feet (1,000 m). Its average high temperature ranges from 77°F (25°C) to 86°F (30°C) in April. In highland villages above 6,562 feet (2,000 m), temperatures can fall near freezing at night.

The highlands have a dry season from November to April. Almost all the highlands' rain falls from May to October. Total yearly rainfall depends on the terrain. Tegucigalpa averages only 39 inches (100 cm) of rain per year. On north- and west-facing slopes, more rain falls.

Honduras lies within an area prone to tropical storms. These storms generally occur between June and November, bringing strong winds and heavy rain. Sometimes the storms develop into hurricanes. Honduras's Caribbean coast is more vulnerable to hurricanes than its Pacific coast is.

Flora and Fauna

Several different kinds of habitat make up Honduras. Unique ecosystems (communities of living things) thrive in each habitat.

Honduran seas support a wide variety of marine life. The reefs and shallows off both coasts shelter plentiful tropical fish, shellfish, sea horses, octopuses, and moray eels. Among these glide huge manta rays and sea turtles. Deeper waters harbor hammerhead sharks, whale sharks, and several kinds of dolphins and whales.

Along many stretches of Honduran coast, palm forests and mangroves grow. Mangroves are shrubs and small trees that flourish in salty water. Fish and shellfish thrive among their sturdy roots. Mangrove swamps also shelter manatees (large aquatic mammals related to elephants) and many kinds of reptiles, such as iguanas, skinks, crocodiles, caimans (a type of alligator), and the deadly fer-de-lance snake. River otters inhabit the waterways of La Moskitia.

Behind the coastal wetlands lie lowland savanna (grassland) and forest. Savanna dotted with pine trees

EPIPHYTES

Honduras is home to many species of epiphytes—plants that grow upon, but do not draw nourishment from, other plants. Epiphytes get moisture and nutrients from the air and rain. They grow abundantly in Honduran forests. They pile up on trees, crowding the branches. During heavy rains, the weight of water stored by epiphytes often becomes too much for their hosts. The great tree limbs crash to the ground and rip out sections of the trunk as they fall.

dominates the northeast. A variety of forest types embrace the other coastal wetlands. Tropical rain forests consist mainly of evergreen trees with broad leaves, such as mahogany and rosewood. Tropical deciduous forests contain trees that drop their broad leaves seasonally, such as the tabebuia (trumpet tree). Dry scrub forests consist largely of thorn trees.

The highlands, too, support a variety of forest types. The western, southern, and central mountains are mainly pine forest sprinkled with oak, scrub, and grassy clearings. The eastern ranges are mostly broad-leaf evergreen forest. Around the highest peaks are cloud forests, a type of rain forest that gets its moisture from persistent mist, fog, and low-level clouds.

Honduras's dense and varied forests are home to a dizzying array of animals. Among the mammals that thrive in Honduras are howler, capuchin, and spider monkeys; large wildcats such as jaguars, cougars, jaguarundis, ocelots, and margays; tapirs (horselike animals with flexible snouts); armadillos, anteaters, and sloths; peccaries (a type of swine); raccoon-like coatis and kinkajous; and colorful birds such as quetzals, parrots, and hummingbirds.

Honduras also has a large amount of cropland and pasture in addition to its natural vegetation. On the slopes of the highlands, small family farms produce coffee, corn, sorghum (a grain), and beans. Some farmers also raise cattle, poultry, and pigs. In the fertile highland valleys and river valleys, large commercial farms produce bananas, sugarcane, and African palm.

Vibrantly colored macaws are a common sight in Honduras. Macaws are a kind of parrot.

Natural Resources

Honduras has many mineral resources. These include antimony (used in flameproofing and electronics), cadmium (used in batteries and pigments), cement, copper, gold, gypsum (used in drywall and plaster), iron ore, lead, limestone, marble, opals, pozzolana (used in cement), rhyolite (a volcanic form of granite), salt, silver, and zinc. However, these resources are mostly untapped. The country's rugged terrain and scarce roads make mining and transport difficult.

Energy resources are limited in Honduras. Though it has some coal and oil reserves, it doesn't extract these fuels. Fuelwood and other biofuels (mainly animal and vegetable waste) provide most of the everyday energy Hondurans use. Sixteen hydroelectric dams supply about one-third of the nation's electricity.

Another key natural resource is land. Honduras's fertile soil and mild climate have made it a productive agricultural nation. Also, many valuable trees—such as pine, cedar, ebony, mahogany, and walnut—are native to Honduras. But logging, farming, mining, fuelwood collection, and wildfire have destroyed much of the Honduran forest. Since 1990 more than 37 percent of Honduras's forest has disappeared.

Environmental Issues

Honduras faces serious environmental challenges. These problems are largely a result of widespread poverty and high population growth.

An ever-growing number of Hondurans require food, shelter, and other means of survival. To supply their needs, many people cut down trees. This not only opens up farmland and pasture, but also provides fuel, building material, and valuable lumber to sell. Trees once blanketed nearly all of Honduras, but today only 42 percent of its land remains forested. Deforestation (clearing trees) continues at a rate of 3 percent per year.

Deforestation has, in turn, led to other environmental problems. Wood burning contributes to air pollution. Heavy farming depletes the soil's nutrients, leading to more clearing as people search for fertile land. Topsoil erodes (washes away) by the ton, choking rivers and estuaries (where rivers meet the sea). Overgrazing by animals makes the erosion worse. Water quality and availability suffer. Landslides and floods increase.

And as suitable habitat dwindles, so does wildlife. Honduras is home to more than 5,600 plant species (kinds) and more than 1,200 animal species. Nearly 3 percent of Honduras's plants and 7 percent of its animals live nowhere else in the world. But many of these species are vanishing. About 130 of Honduran plant and animal species are threatened with extinction (dying out).

Fortunately, both Hondurans and concerned outsiders are aware of these problems and are trying to solve them. Ordinary Honduran citizens have formed a strong movement to preserve their country's environment. The government has set aside nearly 21 percent of Honduran territory as protected land. Public and private groups are setting up programs that address both deforestation and rural poverty. And there's growing support for ecotourism. Ecotourism draws visitors who want to enjoy and help protect Honduran flora and fauna. This type of tourism helps Honduras earn income without destroying its natural resources.

Defender el medio ambiente con dolor

FATHER OF THE FOREST

Olancho Department (state) lies in east-central Honduras. Unregulated logging has destroyed more than half of Olancho's 12 million acres (5 million hectares) of forest. As a result, precious topsoil is quickly eroding, rivers and springs are drying up, water supplies are polluted, and crops are failing.

Powerful landowners, logging companies, drug traffickers, and crime bosses control Olancho's lands. These people have threatened and murdered ordinary citizens who oppose logging. Many citizens have fled.

Father José Andrés Tamayo Cortez (left) is a Catholic priest who serves this region. Tamayo organized the Environmental Movement of Olancho, an alliance of farmers and other residents determined to stop the devastation. In 2003 and 2004, he led thousands of people on two weeklong marches to Tegucigalpa. The marches led to a government investigation of Honduras's forestry agency.

Tamayo has endured harassment and violent assault. Crime bosses have put a price on his head. But still he presses on.

Cities

TEGUCIGALPA (population 765,675) is Honduras's capital and largest city. It lies in south-central Honduras, in a high valley on the Río Choluteca. The Inter-Ocean Highway connects Tegucigalpa with both coasts. Toncontín International Airport offers both domestic and international flights.

Native Hondurans had lived in this area for hundreds of years by A.D. 1500. Lured by the promise of silver and gold, Spanish settlers founded Tegucigalpa in the mid-1500s at the site of a native village. The town remained a mining center for about three centuries. After Honduras gained independence from Spain, its capital alternated between Tegucigalpa and nearby Comayagua until 1880.

Modern Tegucigalpa is the center of Honduran administrative and cultural activities. It houses the national government offices, several museums and art galleries, the National Autonomous University of Honduras, and many beautiful churches. Some of its buildings date from the 1600s.

The city is a local industrial hub. Factories in Tegucigalpa produce textiles (cloth goods), wood products, and many other items. Some silver, lead, and zinc mines still operate on the city's outskirts.

Tegucigalpa is the capital city and cultural center of Honduras.

SAN PEDRO SULA (population 437,798) is Honduras's second-largest city. It lies in the Valle de Sula near Río Chamelecón, a tributary of Río Ulúa. The Inter-Ocean Highway serves this city. So does Honduras's largest airport, Ramón Villeda Morales International. A 32-mile (50 km) railway connects San Pedro Sula with Puerto Cortés on the coast.

The Valle de Sula already contained many towns when the Spanish arrived there. In 1536 Spanish conqueror Pedro de Alvarado founded a town at the site of modern Choloma. The town was an important trade center, where Spaniards collected valuable goods from the interior before shipping them to Spain. After pirates sacked and burned the town in the 1600s, survivors moved their settlement inland to its current location.

The city grew steadily over the next three centuries, then boomed in the early 1900s thanks to the region's thriving banana plantations (large farms for growing cash crops). Though the banana business has declined, San Pedro Sula's population continues to grow. The city remains Honduras's agricultural, commercial, and industrial headquarters. More than two hundred factories operate there.

San Pedro Sula has a small but lively cultural scene. It contains a few historical buildings, museums, churches, and other attractions. Many tourists also visit because the city is near the coast and ancient Maya ruins in Copán.

Visit www.vgsbooks.com for links to websites with additional information about the many things to see and do in Honduras's cities, as well as links to websites about the country's weather, natural resources, plants and animals, and more.

HISTORY AND GOVERNMENT

Near the southwestern city of La Esperanza, archaeologists have discovered stone knives, scrapers, and other tools that are six to eight thousand years old. These artifacts offer clues about ancient Hondurans. The clues suggest that the country's earliest human residents were descendants of the Paleo-Indians.

The Paleo-Indians were northeast Asian peoples who followed a prehistoric land bridge from Asia to northwestern North America. The Paleo-Indian population slowly expanded southward into Central America. These people were nomads at first. They hunted wild animals and gathered plants for food. They eventually developed settled farming societies. When the society made this shift, the Archaic Period began. The people of this period are called Archaic Indians.

Maya Civilization

By about three thousand years ago, Archaic Indians lived all over Honduras. One group settled in a valley alongside Río Copán in west-

ern Honduras, in about 1300 B.C. These people were probably farmers who chose the Valle de Copán for its fertile soil and fresh water. A town developed there. Its residents began making stone buildings about 900 B.C.

In about A.D. 100, newcomers from the north arrived. These people were the Maya. Their society was spreading south from the Yucatán Peninsula (modern Mexico, Belize, and Guatemala). The Maya settled throughout western Honduras in the fertile river valleys. Over three centuries, the Maya gained control of this area.

By 400 the Maya community in Valle de Copán had grown especially powerful. This swampy valley had the perfect climate and soil for growing maize (corn), cotton, and tobacco. The Maya also grew cacao, the source of chocolate. The valley's forests provided jaguar pelts and brilliant bird feathers, both of which the Maya prized. The surrounding hills offered plentiful limestone for construction. A day's walk away lay Río Motagua, Central America's only source of jade.

This pale green precious stone was very important in Maya art and religion. Finally, the valley was well positioned for trade. It served as a route between the Atlantic and Pacific oceans and as a way station for trade among Central American societies.

By the 500s, the community had become a city—and a hub of Maya culture. Twenty to thirty thousand people lived there. Copán bustled with commercial, government, and religious activity. The city's architects built a series of plazas and courtyards surrounded by huge platforms. Sculptures filled the plazas. The platforms supported temples, council houses, and palaces. Carved stone and painted plaster decorated the buildings.

Copán is home to the Hieroglyphic Stairway, the longest Maya text ever discovered. Thousands of glyphs (symbols) carved into stone blocks make up the stairway. The glyphs recount the births, rise to power, important rituals and other achievements, parentage, and deaths of the city's most important rulers.

The driving force behind Maya culture was its religion. In practicing their religion, Maya scholars developed an accurate calendar. Maya scholars were also brilliant mathematicians and astronomers. They invented a number system using dots and bars. They studied and recorded the motions of the sun, moon, stars, and planets. Maya scholars were careful historians too. They developed a complex system of hieroglyphics (picture writing). They engraved hieroglyphics into stone and wrote them in books called codices. These books included family histories of Maya rulers and almanacs that predicted suitable days for planting, fishing, and hunting.

Copán's rulers stopped raising new buildings in 800. Later in the century, the priests and rulers left the city. Meanwhile, Maya civilization was crumbling throughout Central America. Its cities fell into ruin, and its population dropped sharply. Archaeologists don't know why this happened. Whatever the cause, this decline affected only city dwellers. Rural peasants remained in the area. But because these people were uneducated, their descendants either didn't know or couldn't record the details of Maya culture and history.

After the Maya

The Maya population dwindled after 900, but it didn't disappear. The Maya became just one of many native peoples who lived in Honduras. Post-Maya Honduran society was a complex mosaic of cultures.

In the northwest lived the Chortí Maya. These people were descendants of the earlier Maya. Peoples related to the Toltec of central

Mexico settled in southwestern and southern Honduras. The Pipil lived in the southwest, near modern El Salvador. The Chorotega lived in the south, near the modern city of Choluteca.

The Lenca lived in west-central Honduras. These people probably came from northwestern South America. Other South American groups settled in Honduras too. For example, the Jicaque inhabited the western Caribbean coast and north-central Honduras. East of the Jicaque lived the Paya. Along the coast and among the inland swamps of La Moskitia dwelt the Sumu and Tauira.

Borders between peoples were vague. The groups traded and warred with one another for the next six centuries. They also traded with peoples from more distant regions, such as Panama and Mexico. No major cities developed during this time, but the population grew. By 1500 up to two million people lived in Honduras.

Spanish Conquest

In May 1502, Christopher Columbus began his fourth voyage to find a westward sea route from Europe to the Indian Ocean. He landed on the Islas de la Bahía in late July. Two weeks later, he landed on the Honduran coast at Cabo de Honduras (a peninsula, or finger of land, near modern Trujillo). He was the first known European to set foot on the American mainland. Columbus then continued east around Cabo de Gracias a Dios (the easternmost point of Honduras). He explored the Central American coast all the way to Panama before setting out to sea again.

Explorer **Christopher Columbus** appears in this illustration with some of the people he encountered in the Caribbean on his fourth voyage to the Americas.

Hernán Cortés

European explorers mostly ignored Honduras for the next twenty years. Instead they focused on the Caribbean Islands. Then in 1519, Spaniards Gil González Dávila and Hernán Cortés launched explorations of Panama and Mexico, respectively. European interest in Central America revived. The Spanish of Panama and the Spanish of Mexico began fighting over Honduras.

In 1523 González set out to conquer Honduras for Spain. Meanwhile, Cristóbal de Olid set out to do the same on behalf of Cortés. Midvoyage Olid declared independence from Spain. He wanted Honduras's resources for himself. Before long Olid controlled the entire territory.

In 1524 Cortés sent Francisco de las Casas to oust Olid. Instead, Olid gained the upper hand and captured both las Casas and González. But Olid's men betrayed him and freed the prisoners. Las Casas and González joined forces and declared loyalty to Cortés. They went on to establish a Spanish colony headquartered in Trujillo.

The Spanish discovered gold and silver in Honduras in the 1530s. This discovery attracted many Spanish settlers. These settlers soon began fighting over land and mining rights. In 1536 Cortés sent Pedro de Alvarado to restore order in Honduras. While he was there, Alvarado founded the city of San Pedro Sula. In 1537 Alonso Cáceres, another of Cortés's officers, founded the city of Comayagua.

Hernán Cortés sent **Pedro de Alvarado** *(right)* to Honduras in 1536. Eventually Alvarado became governor of both Honduras and neighboring Guatemala.

The gold and silver discovery not only drew settlers, but also increased the need for laborers. To meet this need, the Spanish sought to enslave the Indians. The Indians, though numerous, were no match for Spanish guns, swords, and horses. Fighting the Spaniards, Indians died by the hundreds. Many more became slaves. The slaves toiled on Spanish farms and did dangerous work in the mines. Meanwhile, their Spanish masters grew rich.

Slavery inspired Indian rebellion. In 1537 a young Lenca chief named Lempira led an uprising against the Spanish. Inspired by Lempira, other indigenous groups took up arms too. Revolt swept through western Honduras, and the Indians nearly triumphed. But eventually the Spaniards killed Lempira.

After Lempira's death, the native rebellion faltered. A series of smaller revolts and brutal Spanish crackdowns followed, drastically reducing the Indian population. In 1539 the Spanish controlled about fifteen thousand native Hondurans. Within two years only eight thousand remained.

The Early Colony

Spain managed Honduras's Indian population through the *encomienda* system. An encomienda was a royal grant to an individual Spaniard (an *encomendero*) of a certain number of Indians living in a specific area. The encomendero was supposed to protect the Indians and teach them Spanish. The Spaniard was also supposed to convert them to Catholicism, Spain's official religion. In return he could demand payment from them in gold, silver, crops, or labor. The system did not grant land to Spaniards, but Spaniards typically seized Indian lands anyway. The system was meant to define the free status of Indians and to provide labor for Spanish mines. But in practice it was slavery.

Most encomenderos abused their charges. This mistreatment led to a clash between the Honduran church and the colonial authorities and settlers. Cristóbal de Pedraza, the first Roman Catholic bishop of Honduras, accused his countrymen of ignoring their legal duties and abusing their power. Pedraza worked hard to protect the Indians. But his efforts achieved little change.

As a result of Spanish brutality and European diseases, the indigenous population dwindled. Meanwhile, the Honduran economy grew. Spanish settlers developed cattle ranches and a variety of crops. Mining boomed. To solve the ongoing labor shortage, Spain began shipping African slaves to Honduras in the 1540s. By 1545 about two thousand Africans lived there.

As the Spanish gathered more gold and silver, the Dutch, French, and English pirates prowling the Caribbean grew busier. These pirates robbed ships bound for Spain carrying Central American riches.

They also terrorized Spanish coastal villages. After drinking all the alcohol, they looted and burned the villages.

In the 1560s, new silver strikes in southern Honduras led to the founding of Tegucigalpa. But a lack of tools and labor, rough terrain, the small size of many deposits, and government red tape hampered Honduran mining. In the 1580s, silver prices began to fall. An economic slump followed.

By 1600 Honduras had become a poor and neglected backwater of the Spanish Empire. Its population included a handful of Spanish rulers and landowners and a larger number of Indians, black Africans, and mestizos (people of mixed Spanish and Indian ancestry). Isolated communities were scattered throughout the countryside.

Colonial Honduras

Throughout Honduras's colonial period, mining remained active. It provided most of the tax money Honduras owed Spain. But mining caused constant problems for the Honduran government. Spaniards forced many Indians to move to mining areas—which not only was illegal, but also angered the Indians. Corrupt mining officials constantly tried to avoid paying taxes. Gold and silver smuggling were widespread.

Although mining stayed in the spotlight, agriculture was far more important. Hondurans survived by farming. They raised some products, such as cattle and tobacco, for export. But most people were subsistence farmers. They produced just enough to feed their own families, sometimes with a small surplus to sell.

Colonial development stalled after 1600. Many towns shrank. Some local governments simply shut down. The interior remained largely outside Spanish control. Indians who fled to the hills could govern themselves and preserve their culture. Meanwhile, Spanish culture suffered. Honduras offered little education or art. Poor seaports limited contact with the outside world.

The English posed another major problem. Throughout the 1600s and 1700s, England tried to plant colonies and lumber operations along the Caribbean coast of Honduras. The Zambo and Miskito (Indian-African people of coastal Honduras) helped the English effort. Spanish abuse had made these people willing to attack Spanish settlements. Eventually the English controlled the entire Caribbean coast and islands of Honduras.

In the early 1700s, a new dynasty (ruling family) took over the Spanish throne. The new dynasty helped reduce corruption in Honduras and revive its mining industry. Spain also regained control of Honduras's Caribbean coast and islands in 1786.

Spain allied with France during the Napoleonic Wars (1799–1815). These wars were an effort by Napoleon Bonaparte, ruler of France, to control Europe. In 1808 he ousted the king of Spain. Bonaparte put his brother Joseph on the Spanish throne.

Joseph Bonaparte stepped down in 1813. The Spanish king returned. But the upheaval had weakened the Spanish Empire.

Independence

Honduras left the Spanish Empire without bloodshed. Mexico, Guatemala, El Salvador, Honduras, Nicaragua, and Costa Rica simply declared their independence on September 15, 1821. The weakened empire accepted the declaration in silence.

In 1822 these nations joined to form the Mexican Empire under ruler Agustín de Iturbide. In March 1823, the Iturbide regime collapsed. The Central American nations then declared independence from Mexico. They joined to form the Federal Republic of Central America.

The new federation struggled from the start. Centuries of Spanish rule had nurtured deep divisions among the member states. In addition, the population had split into bitterly opposed political factions: the conservatives and the liberals.

FRANCISCO MORAZÁN

Francisco Morazán (left), a Honduran liberal, was president of the Federal Republic of Central America from 1830 to 1840. He tried to transform Central America into a progressive nation via reforms such as freedom of speech, press, and religion; trial by jury; and equality of all people before the law. Although his presidency ended with the federation's breakup, most Central Americans admire his vision and intelligence. They remember him as a hero and call him "the George Washington of Central America." In Honduras many place-names honor him.

The conservatives wanted an aristocratic, centralized government based on Spanish traditions. They favored policies that gave the church great social power. They wanted to keep Indians in a low social position. The liberals, by contrast, wanted more local freedom and favored separation of church and state. They hoped to develop a U.S.-style democracy (government by freely elected representatives) and a free-market economy. They wanted to integrate Indians into the national society.

The conservative-liberal divide proved fatal to the federation. The Federal Republic of Central America broke up from 1838 to 1840. On November 15, 1838, Honduras became an independent nation.

The rest of the century was chaotic and difficult for Honduras. Its neighbors constantly interfered in Honduran politics. Its liberal and conservative factions continued to wrestle for power. As control of the nation alternated between the two factions, many different military and civilian regimes ruled Honduras.

While Honduran politics roiled, the country remained a social backwater. Honduras had no libraries and no regular newspapers. Schools and cultural opportunities were scarce. The population grew slowly, hovering around four hundred thousand for decades. Tegucigalpa, Comayagua, and San Pedro Sula were the only large towns.

Honduras's economy suffered during this time too. Hondurans hoped mining would brighten their prospects. But the industry had fallen into severe neglect since independence. Many mines were abandoned and flooded. Efforts to

WILLIAM WALKER

In the 1850s, a U.S. citizen named William Walker set out to privately conquer parts of Latin America. He wanted to create slaveholding states ruled by English-speaking white people.

After a failed effort in Mexico, in 1854 Walker led a hired army in Nicaragua's then-raging civil war. He took control of Nicaragua in 1855 and declared himself president in 1856. He then announced a plan to take over the rest of Central America. Guatemala, El Salvador, Honduras, and Costa Rica joined forces against Walker and drove him out in 1857.

In 1859 the United Kingdom (UK)—formerly the Kingdom of England—returned the Islas de la Bahía to Honduras. (The UK had seized them during the federation years.) Some British settlers on the islands asked Walker for help, and he arrived in 1860. But most of the British and all of the Hondurans opposed him. Honduras executed Walker a few days later.

revive mining failed repeatedly due to civil unrest, poor transportation, and poor health conditions.

In 1876 Honduras entered a period of renewal. From 1876 to 1883, Marco Aurelio Soto governed Honduras. He restored order and made basic reforms in finance, education, and public administration. In 1880 he moved the capital permanently to Tegucigalpa. In the same year, he revived the mining industry via a generous agreement with the New York and Honduras Rosario Mining Company (NYHRMC). NYHRMC's gold and silver mine near Tegucigalpa fast became the richest mine in the Americas.

In 1883 Soto resigned. Luis Bográn became president. Bográn built many schools and founded a national press. He attracted foreign investment in agriculture. This investment helped create jobs and develop the northern coast. He improved Tegucigalpa's infrastructure (public works, such as roads). He invited foreign scholars to study Copán.

Bográn lost power in 1891 to Poinciana Leiva. Leiva governed as a dictator (ruler with absolute power), which sparked three years of political and civil unrest. Policarpo Bonilla took power in 1894 and ruled until 1899. Bonilla restored political order, made legal reforms, and improved communications throughout Honduras.

Despite the efforts of Soto, Bográn, and Bonilla, Honduras's economy still struggled. Mining had brought in foreign cash and employed many Hondurans. But all the riches went to the United States. A few Hondurans tried to profit from exporting cattle products, tobacco, and fruit. But the volume of foreign trade stayed small. Most Hondurans continued to survive by subsistence farming.

Banana Republic

Honduras's economy changed drastically in 1899. That year two U.S. fruit companies moved in. A third followed in 1902. United Fruit Company, Standard Fruit Company, and Cuyamel Fruit Company set up banana plantations in Honduras. All three began exporting huge amounts of bananas to the United States.

The banana companies quickly grew very powerful. They forced small farms out of business with land buyouts and threats. The companies soon controlled vast tracts of land, the nation's only railroads, and 80 percent of Honduran exports.

The companies also strongly influenced Honduran politics. To promote their interests, the companies allied with rival parties and military factions. They bribed and pressured government officials. When these tactics didn't work, they financed armed conflict.

In 1914 banana prices began to fall. The same year, World War I (1914–1918) broke out. The Central Powers and the Allied Powers fought each other in Europe. The United States joined the Allies in 1917, turning many of its ships to the war effort. The drop in shipping reduced Honduras's ability to export bananas. It also made imports, such as textiles, scarce. Shortages raised the prices of many goods. Meanwhile, the trade decline cut government income from taxes on imports and exports. Despite its problems, Honduras supported the U.S. war effort and joined the Allies too.

During World War I, banana workers seeking better wages and working conditions formed unions. These unions mounted the first major strikes in Honduran history in 1917 and 1918. In 1920 a general strike hit the Caribbean coast. The United States sent a warship there, and the Honduran government arrested labor union leaders. When one company offered a wage increase, the strike collapsed. But labor troubles continued to simmer.

Throughout the 1920s, the banana companies and the Honduran government coped with constant labor troubles, civil unrest, border disputes, and political chaos. In 1930 the Great Depression (an international economic collapse, 1929–1939) hit Honduras. Banana exports plummeted. Banana companies laid off thousands of workers, cut wages, and lowered the prices paid to independent banana farmers.

The Caríato

Meanwhile, military strongman Tiburcio Carías Andino steadily gathered support. Carías was a clever and ruthless man. He'd begun his military career as a cook and had gradually climbed the ranks to general. Carías won the presidential election in 1932. He ruled for sixteen years. This period became known as the Caríato.

Carías started his presidency by securing his own power. He strengthened the military. He pleased the banana companies by opposing labor strikes. He pleased other nations by paying foreign debts promptly—even though the Depression and banana fungus had crippled Honduras's economy.

Carías also strangled political freedom. He outlawed the nation's Communist party. (Communism is a political and economic theory whose goal is to create equality among people.) He gagged the press. Then he launched a public information campaign stressing that only he could maintain peace and order in Honduras.

By law, the president of Honduras could not serve two terms in a row. So Carías pressured Congress to change the law. Congress did, not only allowing reelection but also making the presidential term longer.

During the Caríato, congressional elections ceased. Congress and the courts were mere tools of Carías, who had become a dictator. He destroyed the unions and imposed military law. He denied women both citizenship and voting rights. He filled the jails with his enemies.

The Caríato was not free, but it was stable. Carías built a skilled military, a large political network, and many new roads. He promoted coffee farming. These achievements helped unify Honduras and paved the way for future modernization and economic development. But social development stalled. Most Hondurans remained poor, isolated, and illiterate (unable to read or write).

World War II (1939–1945) erupted in the middle of the Caríato. The war helped Carías stay in power. The United States supported him because he helped keep Central America stable while the rest of the world was in turmoil.

After the war, Americans could no longer justify supporting Carías. He was a tyrant like those the Allies had defeated in World War II. Hondurans themselves were demanding democracy. U.S. officials persuaded Carías to step down in 1948.

Honduras held elections later that year. Carías' minister of war, Juan Manuel Gálvez, became the new Honduran president.

Modernization

Gálvez continued some Carías policies, such as building roads, developing coffee exports, reducing foreign debt, and favoring the banana companies. But he made some important changes too. He spent more money on education, started an income tax, freed the press, and allowed unions. He also signed laws that slightly improved labor conditions.

COMMUNISM

Communism is a political and economic theory developed in the mid-1800s by German philosophers Karl Marx and Friedrich Engels. Under Communism, a society abolishes private property and works to distribute a nation's riches equally among all its citizens. Individuals give up personal wealth and many freedoms, such as voting rights and the free and public practice of religion. In Communist nations, people do not own their own businesses or homes, elect their own leaders, or make their own political and economic decisions.

Many people around the world have found hope and promise in the Communist ideal of equality. In practice, however, Communism has often not lived up to that ideal. And in the years after World War II, the Communist Soviet Union and the democratic United States were fierce enemies. For this reason, most Americans disapproved strongly of Communism.

Conservatives—mostly upper-class landowners and military leaders—and U.S. companies still ruled Honduras. But infighting weakened their grip on power. Meanwhile, modernization created a Honduran middle class. Members of this class—mostly liberals—wanted access to power. They were furious at foreign political interference. They resented the huge, tax-free profits banana companies made. Working conditions remained dismal on most plantations.

In early May 1954, labor tensions grew into a massive strike. Banana operations ground to a halt. The strike soon spread to other industries. By May 21, nearly thirty thousand workers were striking. The economy was severely strained.

The companies and government insisted the strikers were dangerous Communists. They weren't, but the accusation brought strong U.S. support. (Americans feared the spread of Communism in the years after World War II.) With U.S. help, the companies and government gained the upper hand in strike negotiations.

The strike ended in early July. The settlement favored the companies and government. But fruit companies lost some power in Honduras. And organized labor gained greater influence. This, in turn, led to better labor laws a few years later.

Hondurans elected a liberal president in 1957. Ramón Villeda Morales, a Tegucigalpa doctor, took office in 1958.

In 1958 two-thirds of Honduran adults were illiterate. Half the nation's roads were impassable during the rainy season. The population was exploding. Too many Hondurans relied on too little land to survive. Land scarcity worsened poverty and public unrest. Hon-duras badly needed modernization.

Villeda's government faced the task head-on. He obtained funds from international agencies, the United States, and military spending cuts. Honduras began building highways, schools, hospitals, and clinics. It also began developing domestic industry and agriculture. Congress passed a generous new labor code. A land reform law let the government seize idle land and sell it cheaply to landless peasants.

Villeda's reforms infuriated conservatives. Landowners hated his farming policies. Military leaders resented their loss of power. To make matters worse, another liberal was poised to win the 1963 presidential election. To prevent six more years of liberal reforms, military leaders and wealthy Hondurans overthrew Villeda days before the election.

◎ Military Rule

Colonel Oswaldo López Arellano declared himself president in October 1963. He immediately canceled the election, dissolved Congress, and suspended the constitution.

For the next eighteen years, military officers ruled Honduras. During this period, the government undid many of Villeda's reforms. It harassed the unions. It disbanded liberal organizations. It formed a secret police force to bully political opponents.

As the 1960s wore on, Honduran relations with Nicaragua, Guatemala, and the United States improved. But relations with El Salvador worsened.

The Honduran economy was struggling again. As a result, labor conflicts and political unrest increased. Some Hondurans—including government officials—began blaming the nation's problems on Salvadoran immigrants. About three hundred thousand Salvadorans were living illegally in Honduras.

In 1969 tension between the two countries erupted in a conflict called the Soccer War. The war lasted only four days. But it killed thousands of people, damaged the regional economy, and cut off all relations between Honduras and El Salvador for a decade.

In September 1974, Hurricane Fifi hit Honduras. Massive flooding killed about eight thousand people and destroyed several Honduran cities, most of Honduras's fishing fleet, and half its food crops—including about 95 percent of the bananas. It also led to López's downfall. After Fifi, a banana company reportedly bribed the government to lower banana export taxes. López refused an investigation. The military ousted him in April 1975. Military officers continued to govern Honduras for six more years.

THE SOCCER WAR

In the late 1960s, about three hundred thousand Salvadorans were living illegally in Honduras. The newcomers aggravated the Honduran land shortage. In April 1969, Honduras gave Salvadoran immigrants a month to leave. By June twenty thousand did so.

Meanwhile, the Honduran and Salvadoran national soccer teams met in a three-game qualifying round for the 1970 World Cup. Riots erupted, and two Hondurans died. Exaggerated Honduran news reports led to a wave of violence against the Salvadoran settlers remaining in Honduras. Thousands more Salvadoran immigrants left.

El Salvador responded by breaking off diplomatic relations, sealing its borders, and invading Honduras. The war killed more than two thousand people—mostly civilians. It left thousands more homeless. It damaged the economies of both countries. A state of war between the two nations lasted until they signed a peace treaty in 1980.

Hurricane Fifi caused massive damage and killed thousands of people when it hit Honduras in September 1974.

Caught between Wars

In 1981 international pressure led to fair elections in Honduras. In 1982 liberal Roberto Suazo Córdova became president, ending nearly two decades of military rule. True democracy, however, was slow to return.

In the 1980s, Honduras was caught between two civil wars. In El Salvador, Communist forces were fighting to overthrow the brutal Salvadoran military government. In Nicaragua, a Communist group called the Sandinistas had just triumphed over Nicaragua's long-standing dictatorship. Contras, soldiers opposed to Nicaragua's new government, had fled across the border into Honduras.

Meanwhile, President Ronald Reagan had taken office in the United States. Reagan was determined to thwart Communism in Central America. He believed it threatened free-market democracy throughout the Americas. With Suazo's blessing, Honduras became a tool of the United States. U.S. military staff and intelligence agents used Honduras as a base for training, funding, and arming both the Contras and the Salvadoran Armed Forces.

At the same time, Honduras's own army cracked down on Honduran society. Military hit squads imprisoned, tortured, killed, and "disappeared" hundreds of political opponents, such as labor activists, peasant leaders, and priests. This abuse ended in 1984 with a change in command, but the armed forces still controlled government affairs behind the scenes.

While violence raged around Honduras, the nation became a shelter for refugees. More than two hundred thousand Nicaraguans and twenty thousand Salvadorans fled to Honduras during the conflicts in their homelands.

In the late 1980s, both wars wound down. International peace negotiations played a big role. In addition, the United States grew impatient with funding the conflicts. Salvadorans, Hondurans, and Nicaraguans themselves were weary of the violence and chaos. In 1989 and 1990, new presidents focused on peace and recovery took office in all three countries.

Democracy Returns

Rafael Leonardo Callejas won the 1989 Honduran presidential election. He promised to fix the nation's financial problems. To reduce government spending, the Callejas administration sold many state-owned companies to private buyers. This program did improve the country's finances. But it was hard on ordinary Hondurans. It caused job losses, a wage freeze, and more poverty. In addition, many Callejas officials were corrupt. These problems sparked several public protests against the government.

This **refugee camp in Honduras** sheltered people from El Salvador during violence in the region in the 1980s.

In 1993 Honduran voters elected Carlos Roberto Reina as the new president. Reina promised a "moral revolution." He vowed to end government corruption, reduce military influence, and continue Callejas's economic programs. Honduras saw little economic improvement or reduced corruption. Reina's biggest achievement was placing the military under government control.

Carlos Roberto Flores Facussé won the 1997 presidential election. He promised to modernize the economy and raise the nation's standard of living. Less than a year later, Hurricane Mitch dashed his plans. Flooding from this storm killed seven thousand Hondurans and severely damaged both the natural and human landscapes. It wiped out twenty-five towns, destroyed 80 percent of the country's bridges and roads, and demolished 70 percent of the banana, coffee, sugar, and peanut crops. The hurricane crippled Honduras's economy. Flores estimated that Mitch caused four billion dollars in damage in Honduras and erased fifty years of progress.

The Twenty-First Century

Honduras was starting to show signs of recovery from Hurricane Mitch. Then on September 11, 2001, terrorists hijacked four U.S. airliners and flew them into buildings in New York and Washington, D.C. In total, about three thousand people were killed.

The attacks struck a serious blow to the economy of the United States, a key trading partner of Honduras. The attacks also led to many U.S. security changes. As a result, Honduran tourism—which relied heavily on U.S. visitors—suffered.

Tightened U.S. security included deporting (sending home) larger amounts of illegal immigrants. In particular, Americans ramped up deportation of immigrants charged with crimes. Most immigrants come to the United States from Central America and Mexico. So most of the deported criminals were returned to those places.

These deportations caused a spike in violent gang-related crime throughout Central America, including in Honduras. Honduran president Ricardo Rodolfo Maduro Joest, elected in late 2001, introduced a tough new law to deal with this problem. Maduro's law curbed gang violence and took many gang members off the streets. But it also created government-sponsored abuse. For example, some police joined informal antigang "death squads."

In 2005 Honduras approved the Central America–Dominican Republic–United States Free Trade Agreement (CAFTA-DR). CAFTA-DR reduces Honduran taxes and restrictions on goods, services, and investments from the United States. Supporters hoped it would create jobs and boost the economy in Honduras. Critics worried that large foreign companies would abuse Honduran workers and push small Honduran companies out of business.

José Manuel Zelaya Rosales won the 2005 presidential election on promises to empower citizens, reduce corruption and drug trafficking, and maintain economic stability. He did not fulfull most of his promises. Corruption and drug trafficking continued unabated, and the Honduran economy was fragile. In 2009 Zelaya's approval rating among Hondurans was a low 25 percent.

Manuel Zelaya

Government

Hondurans govern their country by the constitution of 1982. This document divides government powers among the executive, legislative, and judicial branches.

The president leads Honduras's executive branch. The president is both head of state (chief public representative) and head of government (chief decision-making authority). Citizens elect the president to one four-year term by popular vote. Presidential reelection is forbidden.

The Congress of Deputies is Honduras's unicameral (one-chamber) legislature. Citizens elect 128 deputies to four-year terms.

The Supreme Court of Justice leads Honduras's judicial branch. Congress chooses fifteen Supreme Court justices, who serve seven-year terms. The justices hear cases dealing with constitutional questions or international law issues. The Supreme Court is the nation's highest court of appeal. Beneath it are lower courts of appeal, departmental (regional) courts of first instance, and municipal (city) justices of the peace.

Hondurans divide their land into eighteen departments. Departments are regional divisions similar to U.S. states. A governor leads each department. The departments are further divided into 298 municipalities. A mayor leads each municipality.

Voting is mandatory (required by law) for Honduran citizens eighteen years or older. Hondurans consider voting both a right and a duty. However, the law does not penalize nonvoters.

Visit www.vgsbooks.com for links to websites with updated information on Honduras's government.

THE PEOPLE

Honduras is home to 7.3 million people. The population is growing 2.2 percent per year. Researchers expect the population to reach about 12.4 million by 2050—an increase of 69 percent. This is the third-highest growth rate in the Americas.

The Honduran government is concerned about its population growth. In particular, the government sees a connection between large families and poverty. Many parents want to limit family size, but Honduran culture hinders them. The Roman Catholic Church, which frowns on birth control, is influential in Honduras. Men tend to be the family decision makers, and they don't always consider women's desire for some control over childbearing. The government is trying to address these related issues. Its plan to reduce poverty includes promoting equality between men and women and making family planning education and services more accessible.

Honduras's population density is 169 people per square mile (65 people per square km). It's one of the world's least crowded nations

overall. Settlement is denser along the Caribbean coast and in the western and central valleys. Population thins to the south and east.

Since the mid-1900s, the population of Honduras has been changing steadily from rural to urban. In 1950 about 82 percent of Hondurans lived in rural areas, while 18 percent lived in cities. Sixty years later, only 51 percent of Hondurans live in rural areas, while 49 percent live in cities.

▷ Poverty

Honduras is one of the poorest countries in the Americas. More than 50 percent of Hondurans are very poor. They struggle to meet their basic food, clothing, and shelter needs. A smaller middle class struggles to stay out of poverty. A tiny group composes a very rich upper class.

Honduras stands among thirty countries in the world with the greatest gaps between rich and poor. The poorest 20 percent of Hondurans earn 4 percent of the country's income, while the richest

These **homes made of metal** lie on the outskirts of Tegucigalpa. This thatched-roof **mud home** is a typical dwelling in a mountain village in southwestern Honduras.

20 percent of the population earn 56 percent of the country's income. The middle-earning 60 percent of the population make 40 percent of the country's income.

Rural poor people are generally landless or have very small farms. Many Honduran farmers rely on plots that are too small to meet their needs. Productivity is low because of poor soil, steep slopes, erosion, hurricanes, and flooding. Most rural families live in small homes in isolated villages. Scarcity of farmland and jobs drives many rural Hondurans to seek better lives in the cities—especially Tegucigalpa and San Pedro Sula.

Cities offer more opportunity, but many newcomers find that conditions aren't much better there. Rural migrants often wind up in decaying neighborhoods riddled with gang violence. Others end up in urban shantytowns. Shantytowns are settlements of poor people, usually on the outskirts of cities. Their homes are made of scrap material, and they often lack electricity, telephones, running water, or proper sanitation (sewage and garbage removal). Shantytowns tend to be overcrowded. People who live in them suffer from high rates of crime and disease. Honduran shantytowns typically develop on unused hillsides and riverbanks prone to mudslides and flooding.

Health

As a result of widespread poverty, many Hondurans live in substandard housing and suffer from hunger. Poor sanitation and malnutrition often lead to disease.

Diseases that are rare or treatable in many other nations are common—and sometimes fatal—in Honduras. Among these conditions are leprosy and leishmaniasis (severe skin infections) and cholera (a deadly diarrheal infection). Honduras is struggling to control tuberculosis (a lung disease), malaria, and Chagas' disease. Malaria and Chagas' disease are blood infections spread by insects. Medicines that used to work against tuberculosis and malaria are losing their effectiveness. No effective drug or treatment exists to cure Chagas' disease.

Acquired immunodeficiency syndrome (AIDS), a disease caused by the human immunodeficiency virus (HIV), is a moderate problem in Honduras. About 0.7 percent of Hondurans between the ages of fifteen and forty-nine years carry HIV. This is about the same as the HIV rate in the United States.

To slow the spread of HIV during drug use or sex, Honduras has accepted international funds to establish a public education and treatment program. But this program faces strong cultural resistance. The Catholic Church opposes condom use, which is key to preventing the spread of HIV. In addition, Hondurans generally avoid speaking openly about sex, which hampers both prevention and treatment.

Few Honduran women get adequate health care during pregnancy and childbirth. As a result, the nation's rates of infant and maternal mortality are high. In Honduras, 23 out of every 1,000 babies die before the age of one year. For every 1,000 women in pregnancy or childbirth, about 3 die.

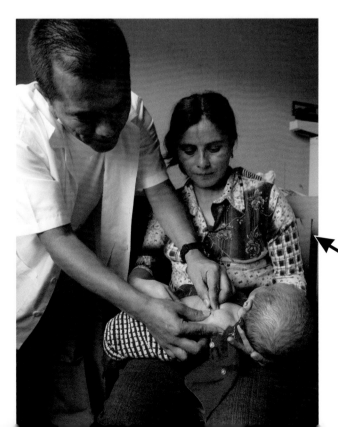

A **health worker** in Honduras gives a baby a vaccination. Health care for pregnant women and babies is not widely available in this country.

The average Honduran can expect to live 72 years. This figure is slightly worse than the average Central American expectancy of 74 years.

Honduras faces a pressing need for better public health systems. These include not only safer drinking water and better sanitation, but also more health-care workers and facilities. Honduras has only 6 doctors and 10 hospital beds for every 10,000 people.

Education

Honduras requires children to attend six years of primary school (elementary school). However, many Honduran children don't receive a full primary education. About 14 percent have no access to schools. And among the poor, many children must work in order to help their families survive.

About 97 percent of girls and 96 percent of boys enroll in primary school. But only 80 percent of girls and 77 percent of boys actually go to school. Among those who attend, 89 percent complete primary school. After that, a student must take a national exam to continue his or her education.

About 71 percent of children who attend primary school enroll in secondary school (high school). Among all Honduran children, only 36

Students attend **primary school** in western Honduras. Primary education is required for six years, but about one-fifth of primary-age Honduran children do not attend school.

Two Honduran **children read in their home,** with their mother and baby sibling watching in the background. Honduras has a high literacy rate despite limited access to education.

percent of girls and 29 percent of boys attend secondary school. At secondary schools, students may pursue different types of education, such as teacher training, technical training, literary and scientific studies, vocational training, or university preparation. Secondary schooling lasts five or six years, depending on the program.

At the end of technical, vocational, or professional secondary school, students earn certificates qualifying them to work in various careers. At the end of university preparation, students take a university admission exam. Those who pass the exam may go on to higher education.

Higher education in Honduras is available at public and private universities as well as at specialized institutes. The public university system includes the National Autonomous University of Honduras, Francisco Morazán National Pedagogical (Teachers') University, and national schools of forestry, agriculture, and music. Honduras is home to nearly twenty private universities and dozens of specialized schools.

Although Honduras has widespread poverty and limited educational access, the Honduran literacy rate is fairly high. About 90 percent of Honduran youths (ages fifteen to twenty-four years) can read and write. About 83 percent of the total adult population can read and write.

Ethnic Groups

Hondurans have a rich mixture of bloodlines. About 90 percent of Hondurans are multiracial. About 7 percent claim purely Indian descent. People of black African heritage make up 2 percent of the population. The remaining 1 percent of Hondurans are white people of European, North African, or southwest Asian descent.

Honduras is home to several large ethnic groups. The Jicaque live in villages dotting Yoro and Francisco Morazán Departments in central Honduras. These villages are isolated from one another. Some still practice ancient Jicaque traditions, such as making cloth from pounded tree bark.

The Chortí Maya live near the Guatemalan border, in Copán Department. These people are descendants of the Maya who built the ancient city of Copán. The Chortí Maya have largely lost their language, traditions, and religion. In addition, wealthy landowners and businesspeople have pushed the Chortí Maya out of the area surrounding ruins of Copán historical park. As a result, they benefit little from the booming tourism there. The government has agreed to give the Chortí Maya a portion of the park entrance fees and redistribute some traditional lands. However, officials have been slow to fulfill this promise.

The Lenca inhabit southwestern Honduras, in a large region embracing the Salvadoran border. They are generally Catholic, but also visit traditional spiritual leaders and practice many of their ancient rituals during community activities such as planting or marrying. Many Lenca wear brilliantly colored traditional clothing.

The Miskito live in La Moskitia along the Caribbean coast and the banks of Río Coco. This ethnic group formed when African slaves fled to the rain forest of La Moskitia and intermarried with the Sumu people. Though this group is both African and indigenous, Hondurans identify it as indigenous. Modern Miskito communities are active in national efforts to protect their environment and people. Many Miskito serve as guides for ecotourists and adventure travelers, such as white-water rafters.

Some people say the name Miskito comes from the word *mosquito* or *musket* (an old-fashioned gun). The Miskito themselves say they descend from a community led by a man named Miskut. In their language, the phrase *Miskut uplikanani* means "the people of Miskut." The Miskito shortened this phrase to *Miskitu*.

The Paya and the Tawahka live mainly in the interior of La Moskitia. The Paya live along Río Plátano, and the Tawahka near Río Patuca. These communities are smaller and more isolated than those of the Miskito. The Paya and Tawahka have preserved their languages and dances. They also still practice traditional crafts, such as making cloth and twine from tree bark and making bows and arrows for fishing.

The Garifuna live along Honduras's northern coast from the edge of La Moskitia to Guatemala, as well as on the Islas de la Bahía. They descend from a community of intermarried African slaves and native Caribbean peoples. Like the Miskito, the Garifuna are both African and indigenous. However, Hondurans identify them as African. The Garifuna maintain a distinct culture that emphasizes music, dance, and storytelling. They follow a religion that mixes Catholic, African, and indigenous beliefs. Because of their difference and their independence, other ethnic groups in Honduras have historically feared and mistreated the Garifuna.

GARIFUNA HISTORY

In 1635 two Spanish ships carrying African slaves sank off the coast of Saint Vincent, an island in the Caribbean Sea. The surviving Africans sheltered with the island's Carib people. The two peoples blended through marriage, creating the Garifuna ethnic group.

When French settlers arrived in the late 1600s, they coexisted peacefully with the Garifuna. But when British colonists and soldiers arrived in the 1700s, war broke out. The French and the Garifuna surrendered to the British in 1796. The British imprisoned about five thousand Garifuna in a concentration camp on the nearby island of Baliceaux.

Half the Garifuna died on Baliceaux. In 1797 the British deported the survivors to Roatán, the largest island in the Islas de la Bahía. The Garifuna prospered there. They established fishing villages and grew cassava (a starchy edible root). Their descendants live today as the Garifuna people of Belize, Guatemala, Honduras, and Nicaragua.

These two girls are part of the Garifuna population of Honduras.

Visit www.vgsbooks.com for links to websites with information on the many ethnic groups in Honduras.

Honduras is home to several smaller ethnic groups too. These include the Chorotega in southern Honduras's Choluteca Department and the Pipil in eastern and central Honduras. Honduras contains the smallest Caucasian population in Central America. Most white Hondurans trace their heritage to British and Spanish colonists or to Arab merchants. They live mainly along the northern coast, on the Islas de la Bahía, and in the large cities.

Social Structure

For all Hondurans—regardless of ethnic or economic status—family is the basic social group. Parents teach their children that relatives must trust, help, and be loyal to each other. People tend to mistrust those outside their family circles.

Hondurans look to their families to understand where they fit in society. Family relationships show them not only where they can seek help, but also where they must give help. In general, family

Families gather together for marriage ceremonies in Honduras, such as this wedding in the Moskitia region.

members with better connections, more power, or higher income are expected to—and do—help less fortunate relatives. Kinship also provides the foundation for formal organizations. Business partnerships and other public alliances work best when they mesh with existing family ties.

Because family is so important in Honduran society, marriage is too. Marrying is a key way to extend or strengthen a family. Both religious and civil unions are socially acceptable. The upper class favors religious marriage, which is a sign of higher status. It usually involves a formal engagement followed by a church wedding and an elaborate fiesta (party). Religious marriage (and divorce) is difficult and expensive, so civil marriage performed by a judge is common among the lower and middle classes.

Within a family, the father is typically an authority figure, and the mother is a nurturer. Males are the traditional breadwinners, but because poverty is so widespread in Honduras, many women add wage-earning work to their household duties. Parents teach their children gender roles beginning early in life. Typically boys get much more physical and behavioral freedom than girls.

WOMEN IN HONDURAS

Honduran law gives women the same legal rights and status as men. Both may vote, own property, and run for public office. But traditional attitudes prevent women's full access to these rights.

Age-old beliefs about women's abilities and their proper role in society have led to widespread discrimination. Career opportunities for women are limited. Working women earn less pay than men doing the same jobs. Women are key players in the Honduran economy—especially in agriculture and service industries. Yet they live in greater poverty than men. Women also are more likely to die from lack of health care.

But conditions for Honduran women are slowly improving. In 1997 Honduras changed its laws to make domestic violence and sexual harassment crimes. In 2000 the government established several public agencies to root out unfair treatment of women in government and business activities. In 2005 women made up about one-quarter of Congress and half of the Supreme Court. Many Honduran women hope that with more attention to their plight and more women in leadership, life for all women in Honduras will change for the better.

CULTURAL LIFE

Honduran culture reflects influences from Central America, Europe, and Africa. Centuries of Indian migration, Spanish colonization, and independent development have created a vivid cultural tapestry in Honduras.

◉ Religion

Honduras has no official religion. The nation's constitution guarantees religious freedom and separation of church and state.

Almost all Hondurans are Christians (people who follow the teachings of Jesus Christ). About 63 percent are Roman Catholics. The Catholic Church is the oldest Christian religious group. It is an international church led by the pope. Catholics believe the pope is the divinely ordained leader of the church. They also believe the pope has the last word on interpreting the Bible and answering moral questions.

Hondurans who aren't Catholic are nearly all Protestant Christians. Protestantism began in the 1500s as an effort to reform Catholicism. It

has since split into many denominations (religious groups) with varied structures and beliefs. Most Protestant churches stress the importance of scripture (Bible texts) over religious leaders. Protestantism appears to be growing in Honduras.

About 23 percent of Hondurans are evangelical Protestants. They belong to about three hundred different churches. These churches focus heavily on preaching and on attracting new believers. The remaining 14 percent of Hondurans belong mostly to other Christian denominations. A tiny number of Hondurans are Muslims and Jews.

Many Hondurans blend Christianity with animism. Animists believe that spirits live in all things—people, animals, plants, and the natural world. Animism also teaches that dead ancestors are spiritually alive. Spirits may be good or evil, and they can affect human lives and events. For animists, keeping the spirits in balance is very important.

CATHOLIC SOCIAL ACTIVISM

In the 1960s, the Honduran Catholic Church began to speak out against the country's unfair government. It denounced military and government abuse of the people—especially poor workers and farmers. In 1975 rich landowners responded by brutally murdering ten peasants, two students, and two priests. The government arrested priests and shut down church-sponsored community organizations. The church retreated briefly in the late 1970s, but then took up the cause of social justice again. It remains a strong voice for ordinary Hondurans in the twenty-first century.

⊙ Language

Spanish is the official language of Honduras. About 95 percent of Hondurans speak it as their first or second language. Honduran Spanish resembles other Latin American Spanish dialects, but it has some unique traits. Honduran Spanish drops certain syllables. It also contains many words borrowed from the Maya language.

About 1 percent of Hondurans—mostly members of the Garifuna ethnic group—speak the Garifuna language. Garifuna mixes the native Caribbean languages Arawak and Carib with Spanish, French, and English.

About 0.5 percent of Hondurans speak English. Most of the English speakers live on the Islas de la Bahía. They are descendants of early British settlers there. The remaining Honduran English speakers live mainly on the Caribbean coast.

This store sign in Puerto Cortés, on the Caribbean coast of Honduras, lists in **Spanish** the different foods available at the market.

Another 0.5 percent of Hondurans speak Miskito. Nearly all are residents of La Moskitia.

The remainder is made up of a few thousand Hondurans who speak indigenous languages such as Paya, Tawahka, and Jicaque. Small handfuls of people speak Lenca and Chortí. Some Hondurans of Arab heritage speak Arabic.

Literature

Honduras has a long, rich tradition of oral literature, or storytelling and spoken poetry. For many centuries, villagers have listened to storytellers at births, weddings, funerals, festivals, and other community events. Storytelling is also a popular evening pastime among elders and children.

Honduran folktales take many forms. Some are jokes, meant for entertainment. Some are stories about historical events and people. Some tales pass along important cultural knowledge. Others teach moral lessons or give advice.

Honduras's diverse ethnic groups share some literary themes. Tales about Spanish colonists, chickens, thieves, and spirits are popular nationwide. Beyond these shared themes, each ethnic group has a unique literary tradition. For example, Garifuna stories often describe activities such as growing cassava, fishing, making canoes, and building baked-mud houses. Miskito stories consist mainly of history and mythology.

Modern (written) Honduran literature was born in the early 1800s, alongside Honduran independence. The first Honduran writer to earn the world's attention was José Cecilio del Valle. Valle was a colonial lawyer, judge, and professor. He gained fame for his ability to reason, argue, and explain. Valle wrote the 1821 Central American Declaration of Independence and coauthored the constitution of the United Provinces of Central America.

José Trinidad Reyes was a Catholic priest in the new nation. He believed the arts and higher education were critical to his country's progress. From 1828 to 1855, he lived in Tegucigalpa. He gave the city

SPEAKING IN HONDURAS

Learn a few simple words in the four main languages of Honduras.

Spanish	Garifuna	English	Miskito
uno	ában	one	kum
dos	biáma	two	wol
tres	úrua	three	yumpa
cuatro	gádürü	four	wol wol
hombre	eyeri	man	waikna
mujer	hiñanru	woman	mairin
perro	aunli	dog	yul
sol	weyu	sun	lapta
luna	kati	moon	kati
agua	duna	water	laya

its first piano, printing press, university, and library. He wrote and staged many *pastorelas* and *posadas* (operas and plays telling the story of Jesus' birth). These works marked the beginning of Honduran theater.

Later in the 1800s, Honduran doctor and feminist Lucila Gamero de Medina wrote the nation's first published novels. Both *Amalia Montiel* and *Adriana y Margarita* (Adriana and Margarita) appeared in 1893. Gamero followed these with many more novels. Her best-known work is *Blanco Olmeda*, published in 1903.

Adults in Honduras often tell duende folktales to frighten children into behaving well. The duende is a mischievous gnome. Sometimes he wanders the forest, whistling beautiful songs to lure young girls. Sometimes he hides in house walls, emerging to clip the toenails—and often the toes—of messy children.

The novel *Prisión verde* (Green Prison), published in 1945, is the most famous Honduran novel. It describes the sufferings of banana workers in the early 1900s. Its author, Ramón Amaya Amador, was a banana worker before becoming a writer. He founded a magazine for workers' rights, wrote more than thirty novels, and published hundreds of political essays and articles during his lifetime.

Roberto Quesada is one of Honduras's top living authors. He founded a literary magazine and has published many short stories. He has also published several novels, including the acclaimed *Los barcos* (The Ships, 1988), *El humano y la diosa* (The Human and the Goddess, 1996), and *The Big Banana* (1999). Quesada often writes about Honduran immigrants in the United States.

Art and Artesanía

Honduran painters are the nation's best-known visual artists. They are famous for their naive art. Naive art tends to use brilliant colors and great detail. It often lacks perspective, which creates the effect of figures floating in space. Naive artists are usually self-taught.

José Antonio Velásquez developed Honduran naive art in the 1950s. With help from a wealthy patron, his paintings reached an international audience. Velásquez's works often show mountain villages with cobblestone lanes winding among white cottages with red tile roofs.

Honduras gave the world many other talented painters too. Muralist (wall painter) Arturo López Rodezno is one. López founded the National School of Arts and Crafts in Comayagüela, near Tegucigalpa. Important Honduran painters also include naive artist

Roque Zelaya and cubists Miguel Ángel Ruíz Matute and Arturo Luna. (Cubists paint forms in a flat, fragmented style.)

Another Honduran artist who has caught the world's notice is cartoonist Dario Banegas. Banegas draws political cartoons for the San Pedro Sula newspaper *La Prensa*. He pokes fun at corrupt leaders and comments on current events. Readers throughout Latin America, the United States, and Europe admire his work. They applaud not only his humor, but also his courage. Social critique in Honduras often leads to lawsuits and political revenge.

In addition to visual art, Honduras has a lively *artesanía* (craft) scene. Honduran artisans, or craft artists, work in many different media and styles. Lenca artisans are famous for their *negativo* pottery. This type of pottery carries black-and-white designs buffed to a high shine. Miskito artisans create *cuadros de tutu* (crafts made from pounded tree bark). Garifuna crafts include baskets and mats woven from a long, slender grass called *nea*. Other popular Honduran artesanía are embroidery, leatherwork, and woodcarving.

Architecture

Home design in Honduras depends on location. In the cities, most people build simple houses with store-bought materials such as brick or concrete.

In the countryside, people build homes with local materials fashioned by hand. Rural homes often have packed-earth floors. Roofs are made of clay tiles or thatch (dry vegetation, such as straw or grass). The walls are adobe (bricks made of sun-dried earth and straw) or wattle and daub. Wattle and daub is a method in which builders weave a frame of wooden strips (wattle) and plaster (daub) it with a sticky material. The plaster is usually a combination of earth, animal dung, and straw. Some Hondurans create wall designs using earth of different colors.

A rural home's kitchen is usually a separate structure outside the house. On the floor or a raised platform is a wood fire. Porches are very common. The porch often circles the house and links the house with the kitchen. Rural Hondurans use their breezy porches like Americans use their living rooms.

A central plaza is the heart of a Honduran town or city. Important government buildings face the plaza. So does a Catholic church. Successful businesses sit on or near the plaza.

Some of the larger cities blend indigenous designs with Spanish ones. For example, in Tegucigalpa, intricate replicas of Maya carvings stand alongside Spanish colonial architecture. These, in turn, contrast sharply with sleek modern skyscrapers.

Music and Dance

Music is an important part of Honduran culture. Music and dance go hand in hand there. In both traditional and modern music, Hondurans generally prefer a lively beat.

Most Honduran ethnic groups have traditional dances and music. The best-known ones belong to the Garifuna. These dances are the *punta* and the *maladio wanaragua*.

The punta began as a ritual performed upon the death of a relative. It has since developed many meanings and uses. Punta dancers swing their hips, move their arms, and take small steps forward and backward. They dance to the throbbing, haunting music of two large drums, maracas (rattles), a conch shell, and a turtle-shell xylophone. The dancers chant as they move, and the audience responds.

The maladio wanaragua depicts the fight of the Garifuna against the British on Saint Vincent Island. The dancers wear painted masks resembling European faces with pencil-thin mustaches. They dance to the music of drums and maracas.

Much of the modern music and dance in Honduras comes from outside the country. Popular styles include Mexican *ranchera* music, Caribbean merengue and salsa, Spanish- and English-language rock and roll, hip-hop, and reggaeton (hip-hop with Jamaican and Latin American influences).

Homegrown pop music is limited in scope. But the local music scene is lively nonetheless.

Punta-rock, a blend of traditional punta and electric guitar, is the most successful type of Honduran pop music. Teenagers and young adults dance the punta to this type of music in all discos around the country.

The best-known Honduran band, Banda Blanca, is a punta-rock band. Its song *"Sopa de Caracol"* ("Conch Soup") topped international Latin music charts in the 1990s. Aurelio Martínez is a rising Honduran punta-rock star.

Marimba bands are very popular in Honduras. A marimba is a type of xylophone with a hollow resonator under each bar. (In Honduras the resonators are usually wooden tubes or hollow gourds.) Around the country, it's normal to hear marimba music at all hours of the day and night.

Honduras is also home to a classical music community. Aspiring classical musicians may study at a number of secondary-level music schools and the National School of Music in Tegucigalpa. Classical music lovers may enjoy the Honduras National Symphonic Orchestra at Manuel Bonilla National Theater in the capital city.

Sports and Recreation

Most Hondurans are poor and work long days. They therefore have little money or time for leisure activities. Hondurans usually spend their limited free time with their families. Common forms of recreation are chatting; listening to the radio; playing cards, chess, and checkers; singing and dancing; and storytelling. On holidays many families visit the beach to swim, sunbathe, picnic, and surf.

Honduran athletes and sports fans are mostly boys and men. Soccer (called football outside the United States) is by far the most popular sport—both to play and to watch. Boys play pickup games whenever they can. Almost every town has a soccer team. Hondurans avidly follow local, national, and international soccer leagues. People listen to big games on the radio.

Basketball is growing popular in Honduran cities. The larger cities have country clubs where wealthy residents can play golf. Sport fishing is another popular activity among rich Hondurans. Private schools may offer basketball, baseball, tennis, or volleyball teams for their students.

Sports for girls and women are not popular in Honduras. While boys play soccer, young girls typically play outdoors with their friends and cousins. They enjoy a circle game called *landa*, in which they push one another and catch their friends' falls. They also play a game like jacks using stones. Older girls spend their evenings with friends. The most popular teen activity on weekends is dancing at the local disco.

Young boys from a Garifuna community listen to their coach while practicing soccer. **Soccer is the most popular sport in Honduras.**

Food

The staples of the Honduran diet are beans and corn. Honduran women grind corn between stones and mix the masa harina (corn flour) with water. They cook the batter on a skillet to make small, thick tortillas. The tortillas are usually eaten warm with fried beans and salt.

Other common foods in Honduras are rice, cassava, and plantain (a type of banana). Eggs and white cheese add protein. Cooks add meat (especially pork and chicken) or fish when they can afford them. Chili peppers lend flavor and spice. Tropical fruits and nuts are plentiful. So are tomatoes, avocados, and many kinds of vegetables. Special-occasion meals feature more meat and fried plantains. Cream enriches both sweet and savory dishes.

Common Honduran beverages take advantage of the country's plentiful fruit. Hondurans make *licuados* (smoothies) with crushed ice, milk, and fruit. Fresh-squeezed *jugos* (juices) made from fruits and carrots are popular too. So are *aguas*, drinks made with water and a fruit or grain.

Adults enjoy drinking coffee. Favorite alcoholic beverages are beer, rum (a liquor made from molasses), *aguardiente* (a vodka-like liquor), *chicha* (a drink made from fermented pineapple skins), and *vino de coyol* (wine made from palm sap).

A Honduran woman **grinds maize** between stones to make corn flour. She will use the flour to make tortillas, a staple of the Honduran diet.

BANANA-BERRY LICUADO

This cooling, refreshing, healthful smoothie is great for a quick energy boost.

1½ cups milk

¾ cup fresh berries

2 tablespoons orange juice

1 teaspoon honey

1 cup ice

1 ripe banana

1. Measure the milk, berries, orange juice, honey, and ice into a blender.
2. Slice the banana into the blender.
3. Cover and blend until smooth. Makes one large or two small servings.

◉ Holidays and Festivals

Honduras's calendar of holidays includes many religious ones. One important religious holiday is the feast day of the Virgin of Suyapa (February 3). The Virgin of Suyapa (a name for Mary, the mother of Jesus) is the patron saint of Honduras. She's believed to have performed miracles in Suyapa, a Tegucigalpa suburb.

Holy Week and Easter (dates vary, in the spring) form another important religious celebration. Throughout the week, families attend church, act out Bible stories, and eat special meals. Many families also picnic at beaches and parks.

Christmas (December 25) is a key religious holiday too. Before Christmas many Hondurans set up nativity scenes (the birth of Jesus) and attend pastorelas and posadas. People go to church on Christmas Eve, then feast with relatives and neighbors well into the night. On Christmas Day, they exchange gifts and light fireworks.

Hondurans also celebrate several national holidays. On Labor Day (May 1), workers march in the cities to show support for one another. Independence Day (September 15) recalls Central America's independence from Spain with parades and patriotic speeches. Hondurans honor Francisco Morazán on October 3. On New Year's Eve (December 31), Hondurans attend church and parties in their finest clothes. At midnight people go outdoors to wish their neighbors well.

Visit www.vgsbooks.com for links to websites that have information on popular foods in Honduras, as well as Honduran recipes.

THE ECONOMY

For nearly a century, the Honduran economy relied almost entirely on banana and coffee exports. But depending heavily on two crops put Honduras at the mercy of rising and falling prices. The two-crop economy also faced great risk from storms and flooding. So around 1990, the Honduran government and private sector (individual business owners) began working together to diversify (add variety to) the economy.

Bananas and coffee are still important. But slowly and steadily, other activities are growing to help balance the economy. For example, Honduras has expanded its agricultural exports to include other products, such as shrimp and melons. It also actively promotes tourism. And Honduras has welcomed many *maquiladoras*. Maquiladoras are foreign-owned factories that bring raw materials and equipment to Honduras tax-free. The factories use these items and Honduran labor to make products for export.

Although Honduras is working hard to stabilize its economy, it has had its ups and downs since the early 1990s. In 1998 Hurricane

Mitch crippled Honduran agriculture. Then the September 11, 2001, terrorist attacks in the United States damaged both foreign trade and tourism.

A few years later, Honduras was recovering—and taking more steps to improve its economy. In 2006 CAFTA-DR took effect in Honduras, amid high hopes of job creation. An international agreement to relieve foreign debt and reduce poverty in Honduras took effect the same year.

But the Honduran economy remains fragile. It still relies heavily on trade with the United States, and therefore suffers when the U.S. economy slumps.

Unemployment in Honduras stood at nearly 28 percent in 2009. Another 10 percent of Honduran workers were underemployed (unable to find adequate work in terms of hours, pay, or skill level). The average annual income per person was about $1,300 —a figure that ranked among the lowest in the world.

◉ Services

Honduras's service sector refers to all business activity that provides useful labor instead of material goods. This sector includes banking, transportation, wholesale and retail trade, business services, telecommunications, hotels, bars, restaurants, tourism, construction, and government services. This sector is responsible for about 59 percent of the nation's gross domestic product (GDP). The GDP is the total value of goods and services produced inside the country in one year. The service sector employs about 40 percent of the workforce.

Honduras's service sector includes many informal businesses. These are businesses that operate without formal structure, organized accounting, or government permits. Because informal businesses are hard to measure, they probably contribute more to Honduran livelihoods than the official statistics suggest. Informal commerce ranges from individual street vendors selling food and household wares to mechanics and repair people.

Honduras is trying hard to develop its formal service sector. Services need few raw materials, tend to provide well-paid and steady employment, and bring in valuable foreign money.

Tourism is the most important Honduran service business. It's a leading earner of income from other nations. Honduran tourism has grown dramatically in the twenty-first century. The government has not yet fully developed and promoted its many scenic and historical attractions. So tourism promises to keep growing.

A **street vendor sells vegetables** at a food stall on Roatán Island.

The biggest current draw in Honduras is the ruins of Copán historical site. Nearly as popular are the reefs along the Caribbean coast, which attract many scuba divers. The country plans to promote its unspoiled beaches, forests, and waterways as ecotourism destinations. By doing this, Honduras hopes to avoid the environmental damage that often follows large numbers of foreign visitors.

Other parts of the service sector are growing too. Among these are telecommunications, construction, banking, and business services.

Industry

Honduras's industrial sector includes manufacturing, mining, and energy. This sector is responsible for about 28 percent of the nation's GDP. Industry employs about 21 percent of the nation's labor force.

Honduran manufacturing long consisted mainly of small plants that supplied domestic needs. To encourage manufacturing and foreign investment, Honduras created free trade zones (FTZs) in the 1970s. In these zones, companies get large tax breaks in exchange for building new factories or for expanding existing ones that produce goods for export.

In 1975 Honduras set up its first FTZ in Puerto Cortés. Since then, hundreds of factories have sprung up in the Puerto Cortés–San Pedro Sula area (the Valle de Sula). As a result, Honduras has greatly increased its output of consumer goods as well as food and beverage processing.

Most Honduran manufacturing takes place in Tegucigalpa and the Valle de Sula. Tegucigalpa plants make plastics, furniture, candles, cotton goods, and leather. Valle de Sula is the center for matches, cigars, cigarettes, cement, meatpacking, sugar, beer, soft drinks, fats and oils, processed foods, shoes, and candles. It is also home to the nation's maquiladoras, which assemble clothing and other textiles. Honduras is one of the top three exporters of textiles to the United States.

Mining accounts for a small portion of Honduran industry. Though Honduran mining is relatively unimportant, the nation does have a variety of mineral resources. These include antimony, cadmium, cement, copper, gold, gypsum, iron ore, lead, limestone, marble, opals, pozzolana, rhyolite, salt, silver, and zinc. However, these resources are mostly untapped. The country's rugged terrain and scarce roads make mining and transport difficult. Honduras does mine enough gold and zinc for export.

Like mining, energy is a small part of Honduran industry. Though Honduras has some coal and oil reserves, it doesn't extract them. Fuelwood and animal or vegetable waste provide about two-thirds of the everyday energy Hondurans use. Imported fossil fuels and domestic hydropower (water power) provide the rest. Sixteen hydroelectric dams supply about one-third of the nation's electricity.

Farmers in Honduras clean their coffee bean crop.

Agriculture

Honduras's agricultural sector includes farming, fishing, and forestry. This sector is responsible for about 13 percent of the nation's GDP. It employs about 39 percent of Honduran workers.

Honduras produces most of its own food. It also exports a large amount of food. Bananas and coffee remain the main cash crop. But other crops became more important in the late 1900s and early 2000s. These crops include African palm (grown for palm oil), sugarcane, plantains, melons, and pineapples. Most plantations lie in the fertile highland valleys and river valleys. Ownership of this valuable land is concentrated in the hands of foreign companies and a Honduran aristocracy (small group of upper-class families). These owners can afford good machinery and seeds as well as many workers.

Small farms on highland slopes grow staple foods such as corn, sorghum, and beans. Some farmers also raise cattle, poultry, and pigs. Families on small farms generally raise food for their own use. They often struggle to survive. Many farmers supplement their incomes with other work.

Along both seacoasts and Honduras's rivers, fishing is an important agricultural activity. Honduras's fish supply is plentiful enough to meet local needs, and sport fishing is a tourist attraction. The nation also has a moderate commercial fishing industry, including refrigerated boats and canneries. Shrimp and lobster are among the most important Honduran agricultural exports. Commercial fishing boats also haul in large amounts of snapper, grouper, and mackerel.

Up to 85 percent of timber produced by Honduras is harvested illegally. This illegal trade weaves a wide web of corruption that includes government officials, timber companies, police officers, landowners, crime bosses, and drug traffickers.

Many valuable trees—including various pines and hardwoods such as cedar, ebony, mahogany, and walnut—

are native to Honduras. But agriculture, mining, forest fires, and illegal logging have destroyed 58 percent of Honduras's native forest. Deforestation continues at a rate of 3 percent per year. To stem this damage, the government has set aside nearly 21 percent of Honduran territory as protected land. Honduras is also cracking down on illegal logging. Public and private organizations are establishing programs that support sustainable use of forest products. These programs help poor Hondurans use forest resources without destroying them.

Foreign Trade

Honduras imports more goods than it exports. Imports such as machinery, vehicles, industrial raw materials, chemicals, fuels, wheat, and rice are responsible for 62 percent of Honduras's foreign trade. Exports such as clothing, coffee, fruit, shellfish, gold, palm oil, and lumber account for about 38 percent of foreign trade.

About one million Honduran citizens live abroad, mainly in the United States. They send home about two billion U.S. dollars per year. These remittances are a big part of Honduras's export income. In effect, the country exports labor to earn foreign cash.

Honduras's most important trading partner is the United States. About 41 percent of Honduran import business and 35 percent of export business is with the United States. Other key trading partners are El Salvador, Guatemala, Mexico, Nicaragua, and Costa Rica.

Transportation

The road system of Honduras has improved greatly since the mid-1990s. It has grown from about 2,000 miles (3,219 km) of highway to 9,570 miles (15,400 km). About 1,942 miles (3,125 km) of these roadways are paved.

The Inter-Ocean Highway is a key transport and travel artery. It connects Tegucigalpa with both coasts and with San Pedro Sula. Many feeder roads connect outlying regions to this highway. The Pan-American Highway crosses Honduras, but just barely. It enters from El Salvador near the Gulf of Fonseca and runs about 100 miles (160 km) to the Nicaraguan border.

Rail service exists only in the north, connecting the industrial and banana-growing zones with the main ports and coastal cities. The National Railway of Honduras, owned and operated by the government, maintains all 434 miles (699 km) of track. Tegucigalpa has no rail service, and Honduras has no international rail connections.

Aviation plays a vital role in linking Honduran communities, especially in the highlands and La Moskitia, where roads are poor and scarce. Honduras has 112 airports. Twelve of these have paved runways. The two main airports are Ramón Villeda Morales International in San Pedro Sula and Toncontín International in Tegucigalpa.

Four large seaports—Puerto Cortés, Tela, La Ceiba, and Puerto Castilla—serve the Caribbean coast. Another Caribbean port, Roatán, lies offshore on the Islas de la Bahía. Puerto de Henecán lies on the Pacific coast. La Ceiba and Tela are primarily banana-trade ports; Puerto Castilla serves the lumber trade. Puerto Cortés and Puerto de Henecán handle general traffic. River traffic is negligible. Most Honduran waterways are navigable only by small boats.

▶ Communications

Honduras's communication services are limited. Few households own landline telephones, although urban areas offer public phone service. Honduras has about one landline phone per ten people. Mobile phone use is growing quickly. Honduras has about six cellular phones per ten people.

Most private homes don't have computers or Internet access. However, both are available to city dwellers via Internet cafés. Honduras has about 424,200 Internet users.

Honduras's constitution guarantees freedom of the press. The government doesn't generally respect this right, though. The media itself is also highly political and corrupt. The nation has four main newspapers. *La Tribuna*, *El Heraldo*, and *El Tiempo* are all published in Tegucigalpa. *La Prensa* is published in San Pedro Sula.

Television use is rare. Honduras has only about one television per

DRUG TRAFFICKING

Honduras has a serious drug trafficking (trade) problem. Colombian cocaine smugglers use Honduras as a stopover when shipping drugs to the United States.

Most of the smuggling happens at sea. Honduras's Caribbean coast is sparsely settled and poorly policed. Honduran drug organizations based there use small boats to help Colombian organizations move cocaine northward. Some drug shipments travel through Honduras along the Pan-American Highway. Other drug shipments arrive by small planes that land on isolated Honduran roads. The drugs then travel north by truck.

In February 2008, President Zelaya proposed legalizing drug use—not only in Honduras, but throughout Central and North America. He said that doing so would free up government resources, weaken drug smugglers, and reduce violent crime. Honduras suffers an average of ten murders per day, seven of which result from the international drug trade.

Tourist attractions, such as this hotel on the northern coast of Honduras, will be important to the country's economy in the future. Visit the website at www.vgsbooks.com for links to more information on visiting Honduras.

ten people. Radios are far more common. About half of Hondurans have one. For those who can afford radios and televisions, Honduras has about three hundred radio stations and eleven television stations.

The Future

The early twenty-first century proved to be a difficult time for many Hondurans. The nation struggled to recover from Hurricane Mitch and adapt to the international changes after September 11, 2001. Its unemployment rate and foreign debt skyrocketed.

The government is taking steps to increase foreign investment while creating jobs in export manufacturing. It has also begun a program aimed at reducing both foreign debt and poverty. Tourism promises to be a great new source of income too.

But Honduras has a difficult road ahead. Certain key obstacles are outside Honduran control. Lower demand for Honduran exports and tight credit throughout the world pose big challenges. Hondurans will have to work harder than ever, and their leaders will need to think and act boldly.

Fortunately, Hondurans have shown repeatedly that they can survive and recover when disaster—both natural and human—strikes. Peaceful civilian government and economic development since the late 1980s may not have brought great material benefits, but they have prepared Honduras for the struggles ahead. With wise use of its valuable resources, Honduras has high hopes for a bright future.

Timeline

6000–4000 B.C.	Paleo-Indians live in southwestern Honduras.
CA. 1300 B.C.	Farmers begin settling in a valley alongside Río Copán.
1000 B.C.	Farmers called Archaic Indians live all over Honduras.
CA. 900 B.C.	Residents of Valle de Copán begin making stone buildings.
A.D. 100–400	The Maya gain control of western Honduras.
400–500	The Maya community in Valle de Copán develops into a city.
500–800	The city of Copán is a hub of Maya culture.
800–900	Maya civilization crumbles.
900–1500	A complex mosaic of cultures develops all over Honduras.
1502	Christopher Columbus explores Honduras.
1520s and 1530s	Spaniards discover gold and silver and establish settlements in Honduras.
1536	Spanish conqueror Pedro de Alvarado founds the city of San Pedro Sula.
1537–1539	Lenca chief Lempira leads an Indian rebellion.
1540s	Spain begins shipping African slaves to Honduras.
1560s	Spaniards found the city of Tegucigalpa.
1580s	Mining problems and falling prices cause an economic slump.
1600s	Honduras suffers from Spanish neglect. England tries to colonize the coast.
1700s	Honduran mining revives.
1786	Spain reclaims control of the Honduran coast and islands.
1821–1822	Honduras, Mexico, Guatemala, El Salvador, Nicaragua, and Costa Rica together declare independence from Spain and join the Mexican Empire.
1823	The Mexican Empire collapses. Honduras, Guatemala, El Salvador, Nicaragua, and Costa Rica form the Federal Republic of Central America.
1838–1840	The federation breaks up. Honduras becomes independent.
1880	President Marco Aurelio Soto establishes a permanent capital in Tegucigalpa. He also signs an agreement with the New York and Honduras Rosario Mining Company.

LATE 1880s   President Luis Bográn invites foreign scholars to study Copán.

1899-1902   Three U.S. fruit companies set up banana plantations in Honduras.

1914-1918   World War I takes place in Europe. Honduras joins the Allies in 1917.

1929-1939   The Great Depression occurs around the world.

1932   Military strongman Tiburcio Carías Andino becomes president of Honduras.

1948   Carías steps down under U.S. pressure.

1954   Thirty thousand Honduran workers mount a massive strike.

1958   President Ramón Villeda Morales takes office and makes drastic reforms.

1963   Military leaders and wealthy Hondurans overthrow Villeda.

1969   Honduras and El Salvador fight the Soccer War.

1974   Hurricane Fifi hits Honduras, killing eight thousand people and crippling the economy.

1981   Hondurans vote in the nation's first free and fair elections since 1957. They elect Roberto Suazo Córdova as president.

MID-1980s   Honduras is caught between El Salvador's and Nicaragua's civil wars. The United States uses Honduras as a base to thwart Communist forces in both wars. Hondurans suffer a military crackdown. Honduras shelters 220,000 Salvadoran and Nicaraguan refugees.

EARLY 1990s   Central American wars end.

1990s   Honduras begins balancing its agricultural economy with more manufacturing and tourism.

1998   Hurricane Mitch hits Honduras, killing seven thousand people and destroying the economy.

2001   Terrorist attacks in the United States cause a drop in U.S. trade with and tourism to Honduras.

2003-2004   Father José Andrés Tamayo Cortez leads thousands of Hondurans on weeklong marches to protest illegal logging.

2005   Honduras approves the Central America-Dominican Republic-United States Free Trade Agreement.

2006   CAFTA-DR takes effect in Honduras. President José Manuel Zelaya Rosales takes office.

2008   President Zelaya proposes legalizing drug use throughout Central and North America.

2009   National elections are slated for November.

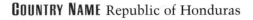
COUNTRY NAME Republic of Honduras

AREA 43,278 square miles (112,090 square km)

MAIN LANDFORMS Highlands (Cordillera del Merendón, Sierra de Puca-Opalaca, Sierra de Montecillos, Montañas de Comayagua, Montañas de la Flor, Cordillera Nombre de Dios, Sierra Río Tinto, Sierra de Agalta), Pacific Lowlands, Caribbean Lowlands, Valle de Sula

HIGHEST POINT Cerro de las Minas, 9,349 feet (2,850 m) above sea level

LOWEST POINT Sea level

MAJOR RIVERS Río Coco, Río Patuca, Río Ulúa, Río Choluteca

ANIMALS anteaters, armadillos, caimans, capuchins, coatis, cougars, crocodiles, dolphins, fer-de-lance snakes, hammerhead sharks, howler monkeys, hummingbirds, iguanas, jaguars, jaguarundis, kinkajous, manatees, manta rays, margays, moray eels, ocelots, octopuses, parrots, peccaries, quetzals, river otters, sea horses, sea turtles, skinks, sloths, spider monkeys, tapirs, whale sharks, whales

CAPITAL CITY Tegucigalpa

OTHER MAJOR CITIES San Pedro Sula, Puerto Cortés

OFFICIAL LANGUAGE Spanish

MONETARY UNIT Lempira.
100 centavos = 1 lempira.

HONDURAN CURRENCY

Honduras's currency is the lempira. Its international currency code is HNL, and its written symbol is L. The government introduced the lempira in 1931. Its name honors the sixteenth-century Lenca chief Lempira. His picture adorns both the 1-lempira bill and the 50-centavo coin. Coins come in denominations of 5, 10, 20, and 50 centavos. Paper notes come in denominations of 1, 2, 5, 10, 20, 50, 100, and 500 lempiras.

Honduras adopted its flag in 1866. The flag displays three equal horizontal bands of blue, white, and blue. In the middle of the white band are five blue stars arranged in an X shape. The blue stripes symbolize the two oceans embracing the land of Honduras, symbolized by the white stripe. The stars represent the five other members of the former Federal Republic of Central America.

"Tu Bandera Es un Lampo de Cielo" ("Your Flag Is a Heavenly Light") is the national anthem of Honduras. Honduran poet Augusto Constancio Coello wrote the lyrics. Composer and music teacher Carlos Hartling, a German-born immigrant to Honduras, composed the music. Honduras adopted this anthem in 1915. The lyrics appear below in English.

Your Flag Is a Heavenly Light
Your flag is a splendor of sky
Crossed with a band of snow;
And there can be seen, in its sacred depths,
Five pale blue stars.
In your emblem, which a rough sea
With its wild waves protects,
Behind the bare summit of a volcano,
A star brightly shines.

To guard this divine emblem
We shall march, oh fatherland, to the death;
Our death will be honored
If we die thinking of your love.
Having defended your holy flag,
And shrouded in its glorious folds,
Many, Honduras, shall die for you,
But all shall fall with honor.

For a link to a site where you can listen to Honduras's national anthem, "Your Flag Is a Heavenly Light," visit www.vgsbooks.com.

TIBURCIO CARÍAS ANDINO (1876–1969)

Carías was a twentieth-century Honduran dictator. He was born in Tegucigalpa. In 1891 Carías began fighting for liberal political and military causes. He earned a law degree in 1898 and worked as a teacher for several years. He left the liberals in 1903 to help found the conservative National Party of Honduras. He became a general in 1907 and spent the next two decades building political and military support. In 1932 he won the presidency. His sixteen-year rule brought order and stability but also strangled civil rights. He stepped down in 1948 under U.S. pressure. He remained powerful in the National Party until his death in Tegucigalpa.

AMERICA FERRERA (b. 1984)

Ferrera is a popular Honduran American actress. She was born in Los Angeles, California, to Honduran immigrants. She acted in school plays and community theater throughout her childhood. In 2002 she debuted on the big screen as the lead character in *Real Women Have Curves*. This film won seven awards—one of them for Ferrera's performance. Since then, she has landed many screen, stage, and television roles. Among these are her award-winning roles as Carmen in the film *The Sisterhood of the Traveling Pants* and as Betty in the television series *Ugly Betty*.

LUCILA GAMERO DE MEDINA (1873–1964)

Gamero was an acclaimed Honduran novelist. She was born in Danlí to an upper-class—though not rich—family. She was a practicing doctor and pharmacist in addition to being an outspoken feminist and a prolific novelist. Her first published stories appeared in 1893. Her novel *Blanco Olmeda* (1903), considered her masterpiece, was the first published Honduran novel. The Catholic Church excommunicated (banished) her for criticizing the clergy in this book.

LEMPIRA (late 1400s–1537)

Lempira was a Lenca chief who led a rebellion against the Spaniards in the late 1530s. Little is known about his life, and historical records of his death disagree with one another. In 1537 Lempira commanded either thousands or tens of thousands of native Hondurans during a widespread uprising against the Spanish. Amid the fighting, Lempira and his followers sheltered on a fortified hilltop called Cerquín in western Honduras (near the modern city of Gracias). He died there—either during a Spanish ambush or in full combat.

FRANCISCO MORAZÁN (1792–1842)

Morazán was a military leader and liberal statesman during the period when Central America gained independence from Spain. He was born in Tegucigalpa to an upper-class colonial family. He educated himself in history, language, and military strategy. He learned about law and government working for

Tegucigalpa's mayor. He joined the military in 1821 and rose quickly through the ranks. He served as president of the Federal Republic of Central America from 1830 through its collapse (1838–1840). After two years of exile, his supporters betrayed and executed him in Costa Rica. Central Americans remember him as a brilliant visionary.

JOSÉ ANTONIO VELÁSQUEZ (1906–1983) Velásquez was a famous Honduran painter. He was born in the village of Caridad in southern Honduras and settled in the town of San Antonio de Oriente. He worked as the barber at the Pan-American School of Agriculture in nearby Zamorano. He was a self-taught painter who developed Honduran naive art in the 1950s. His work inspired a Honduran art boom in the 1960s and 1970s. With the help of Wilson Popenoe, founder of the Zamorano school, Velásquez reached a worldwide audience. He is best known for his paintings depicting life in and around San Antonio de Oriente.

RAMÓN VILLEDA MORALES (1909–1971) Villeda was president of Honduras from 1958 to 1963. He was born in Nueva Ocotepeque in western Honduras. He studied medicine in Tegucigalpa and Germany. In 1940 he returned to Honduras to practice medicine and help rebuild the Liberal Party of Honduras. He became president of Honduras in 1958 after twenty-six years of conservative rule. He made sweeping reforms in military spending, agriculture, infrastructure, labor, public health, and education. He was beloved by ordinary Hondurans but hated by military leaders and wealthy landowners. The latter overthrew Villeda in 1963. He later led the Honduran delegation to the United Nations. He died in New York City.

CELAQUE MOUNTAINS NATIONAL PARK Celaque Mountains National Park in western Honduras is one of the nation's most impressive nature preserves. It consists entirely of lush, steep cloud forest. It boasts Cerro de las Minas, Honduras's highest peak. The park contains eleven rivers and a majestic waterfall. Celaque is also home to 232 plant species, 48 kinds of mammals, 269 bird species, and 18 kinds of reptiles. Hikers sometimes spot jaguars, pumas, ocelots, spider monkeys, and quetzals.

RUINS OF COPÁN Ruins of the ancient Maya city of Copán lie in the Copán Ruins Archaeological Park, adjacent to the town of Copán Ruinas. Copán is one of the most important sites of the Maya civilization. Its ruined citadel and imposing public squares reveal the three main stages of development before the city was abandoned in the early 900s. The United Nations Educational, Scientific, and Cultural Organization (UNESCO) has named Copán a World Heritage Site for its value to humankind.

LAGO DE YOJOA Lago de Yojoa is Honduras's largest and most beautiful natural lake. Towering mountains surround it. These mountains contain two national parks: Cerro Azul Meámbar and Santa Barbara. Within the latter lies Honduras's second-highest peak, Montaña Santa Barbara. Lago de Yojoa is a favorite among bird-watchers, who have identified more than 375 species along its shores. It is also a hiking and bass-fishing hot spot. Nearby Los Naranjos is home to a Lenca eco-archaeological park.

RÍO PLÁTANO BIOSPHERE RESERVE The Río Plátano Biosphere Reserve is one of the largest protected areas in Central America. Like Copán, it is a UNESCO World Heritage Site. It includes undisturbed rain forest, coastal lagoons, beaches, mangroves, grasslands, and pine savanna. The region hosts abundant wildlife, such as manatees, crocodiles, monkeys, tapirs, and toucans. It is home to Miskito and Garifuna people who live much as they have for centuries. The region has very few roads; most travel is by boat and on foot. About 6 miles (10 km) upstream from the mouth of the Río Plátano lies the village of Las Marias, where visitors can see thousand-year-old petroglyphs (rock carvings).

ROATÁN Roatán is the largest and most popular of the Islas de la Bahía. A rich living reef surrounds the island, making it a paradise for divers and snorkelers. The clear turquoise waters abound with colorful tropical fish and other interesting marine wildlife. The island itself is home to botanical gardens, butterfly and iguana farms, family recreational areas, forest canopy tours, and picturesque villages, beaches, and bays.

animism: a system of belief in spirits that inhabit natural places, beings, things, and the everyday world, and which influence human lives and fortunes

cassava: a root plant that is a staple of the Honduran diet; also called manioc

colony: a territory controlled by a foreign power

Communism: a political and economic theory supporting community ownership of all property. Its goal is to create equality.

conservatives: people who support established institutions and cultural norms and who generally favor a limited role for government. In political spheres, conservatives are often called the right.

constitution: a document defining the basic principles and laws of a nation

deforestation: the loss of forests due to logging or clearing land for human uses. Deforestation leads to soil erosion, loss of wildlife habitat, and global warming.

democracy: government by the people through free elections

dictatorship: a form of government in which one ruler or a very small group of rulers has absolute power

gross domestic product (GDP): the total value of goods and services produced inside a country over a period of time, usually one year

hydroelectric power: electricity produced by damming a river and then harnessing the energy of rushing water at hydroelectric power stations

inflation: a persistent rise in prices

infrastructure: a system of public works, such as roads, power lines, and telephone lines

liberals: people who support the idea that institutions and cultural norms can change as societal attitudes shift and who generally support a broad role for government. In political spheres, liberals are often called the left.

literacy: the ability to read, write, and do basic math

nomad: a person who moves from place to place in search of pasture and water for livestock or in search of better hunting grounds

plantations: large farms producing cash crops, such as bananas or coffee

sorghum: a grass related to sugarcane, grown as a grain in Honduras. Sorghum is a staple of the Honduran diet.

Chandler, Gary, and Liza Prado. *Honduras and the Bay Islands.* **Oakland, CA: Lonely Planet Publications, 2007.**
This travel guide provides in-depth information on Honduras's wide array of natural and historical landmarks, as well as on contemporary Honduran culture. The book also includes a summary of the country's history and politics.

Dussel, Enrique. *A History of the Church in Latin America: Colonialism to Liberation.* **Grand Rapids, MI: William B. Eerdmans Publishing, 1981.**
This history examines the development of Catholic Christianity in Central and South America, the Caribbean, and the southwestern United States. It explores the ways in which the New World and Christianity affected each other.

Euraque, Darío A. *Reinterpreting the Banana Republic: Region and State in Honduras, 1870–1972.* **Chapel Hill, NC: University of North Carolina Press, 1996.**
This book explains why Honduras escaped the pattern of revolution and civil wars suffered by its neighbors Guatemala, El Salvador, and Nicaragua. The author challenges the widely accepted idea that multinational corporations completely controlled Honduran politics. Instead, he demonstrates how local society on Honduras's northern coast influenced national political development.

Gordon, Raymond G. *Ethnologue: Languages of the World*, **15th ed. Dallas: SIL International, 2005.**
This book is a window on Honduras's diverse and numerous ethnic groups. It provides detailed descriptions of the many languages and dialects spoken in Honduras, including locations, alternate names, classifications, and maps. It also directs readers to many other publications, such as dictionaries and scholarly articles, that discuss Honduran languages and cultures.

Humphrey, Chris. *Honduras.* **Berkeley, CA: Avalon Travel Publishing, 2006.**
This volume in the Moon Handbooks series is a travel guide and more. It details not only Honduras's many tourist attractions, but also the nation's land, history, government, culture, and people. The book is extensively researched, engagingly written, and filled with helpful maps and sidebars.

Merrill, Tim. *Honduras: A Country Study.* **Washington, DC: U.S. Government Printing Office, 1995.**
This is a comprehensive handbook on Honduras that gives background on the nation's geography, climate, history, economy, society, political affairs, and culture.

Population Reference Bureau. **February 19, 2009.**
http://www.prb.org (March 8, 2009)
The bureau offers current population figures, vital statistics, land area, and more. Special articles cover the latest environmental and health issues that concern each country.

Selected Bibliography

Schulz, Donald E., and Deborah Sundloff Schulz. *The United States, Honduras, and the Crisis in Central America.* **Boulder, CO: Westview Press, 1994.**

This book describes Honduran politics as well as the personalities, motives, and actions of both Honduran and U.S. policy makers to shed light on Honduras in the 1980s. The authors show how Honduras's relationship with the Reagan administration was often a tale of intrigue, violence, and corruption.

Sharer, Robert J., and Loa P. Traxler. *The Ancient Maya.* **Palo Alto, CA: Stanford University Press, 2006.**

This book traces the evolution of Maya civilization from 1000 B.C. to A.D. 1500. Chapter by chapter, it explains the major events in Maya history. Then it examines every major aspect of Maya life. It incorporates all the latest archaeological evidence and historical studies, offering a comprehensive and up-to-date study of this important society.

Soluri, John. *Banana Cultures: Agriculture, Consumption, and Environmental Change in Honduras and the United States.* **Austin, TX: University of Texas Press, 2005.**

In this book, Soluri studies the Honduran banana industry and the U.S. consumer market from 1870 to the present. He sheds light on Honduras's complex modern history and shows how export agriculture has affected the Honduran people, economy, and environment.

UNICEF: Honduras. **2009.**
http://www.unicef.org/infobycountry/honduras_statistics.html **(March 8, 2009)**

This website of the United Nations Children's Fund provides news updates, real-life stories, and statistics on population, health, education, and other issues affecting the lives of children in Honduras.

The World Factbook. **March 5, 2009.**
https://www.cia.gov/library/publications/the-world-factbook/geos/ho.html **(March 8, 2009)**

This website features up-to-date information about the people, land, economy, and government of Honduras. It also briefly covers transnational issues.

World Health Organization: Honduras. **2009.**
http://www.who.int/countries/hnd/en **(March 8, 2009)**

This website offers the latest news and statistics on health issues in Honduras.

BBC News Country Profile: Honduras
http://news.bbc.co.uk/2/hi/americas/country_profiles/1225416.stm
This helpful site provides a quick overview of Honduras's recent history, political events, and economic development.

Behnke, Alison. *Cooking the Central American Way.* **Minneapolis: Lerner Publications Company, 2005.**
The cuisines of Central America—including Honduras—are featured in this cultural cookbook that also looks at the land and customs of the region.

Day, Nancy. *Your Travel Guide to the Ancient Mayan Civilization.* **Minneapolis: Twenty-First Century Books, 2001.**
Take a trip back in time to visit life among the ancient Maya.

DiPiazza, Francesca Davis. *El Salvador in Pictures.* **Minneapolis: Twenty-First Century Books, 2008.**
This book examines El Salvador's history, society, and culture, including its interactions with Honduras.

Gold, Janet N. *Culture and Customs of Honduras.* **Westport, CT: Greenwood Press, 2009.**
This comprehensive book for high school students explores modern Honduran life and culture. Key elements of discussion are national identity, cultural diversity, and indigenous Honduras. The book also examines religion, daily routines, food, dress, media, sports, festivals, literature, crafts, visual arts, music, and dance.

Honduras: Cultural Profiles Project
http://www.cp-pc.ca/english/honduras
This easy-to-read website is loaded with information, photos, and interesting trivia on Honduran culture. The University of Toronto and Immigration Canada sponsor this website to educate Canadians who mentor Honduran immigrants to Canada.

Honduras This Week
http://www.hondurasthisweek.com
Honduras This Week is an electronic newspaper in English. It provides up-to-the-minute news on happenings in Honduras, as well as on topics of interest to Hondurans at home and abroad.

Land Scape Regional Guide and Map of Honduras
http://www.cityofnanaimo.com/CAmerica/Honduras/HondurasRd.pdf
This website offers an extremely detailed map of Honduras. The map labels all Honduran rivers, lakes, roads, mountains, nature preserves, airports, and communities from the tiny and isolated to the large and well-known. It also provides a site map of the ruins of Copán and a street map of Tegucigalpa. The map can be used online or downloaded for free. Users can search the map electronically for geographical names and terms.

Lonely Planet: Honduras
http://www.lonelyplanet.com/honduras
This handy online traveler's guide gives up-to-date information on conditions within Honduras, summarizes the nation's culture and background, and guides travelers to notable parks, historic sites, beaches, islands, and cities.

Further Reading and Websites

McGaffey, Leta. *Cultures of the World: Honduras*. Tarrytown, NY: Marshall Cavendish, 1999.

In this book for young adults, the author reviews Honduras's history and culture, giving a wealth of details on the various ethnic groups living within the country and their art, writing, food, recreation, holidays, and traditions.

Nazario, Sonia. *Enrique's Journey*. New York: Random House, 2007.

Enrique's mother left him in Honduras when he was five years old. She planned to work hard in the United States, save money, then move back home. But twelve years later, she was still wiring money home. That's when Enrique decided to join her. In this book for high school students, Nazario retraces Enrique's northward journey on top of trains, hitchhiking, taking buses, facing horrific dangers, and eventually reuniting with his mother, who has become a stranger. This story won two Pulitzer prizes when it first appeared in the *Los Angeles Times*.

Nova Online: Lost King of the Maya
http://www.pbs.org/wgbh/nova/maya

This website is a companion to the public television program *Lost King of the Maya*. It offers a video tour of Copán, U.S. journalist John Lloyd Stephens's account of discovering Copán in 1839, a map of the Maya world, and an interactive page challenging users to decipher Maya hieroglyphs.

Rohmer, Harriet, and Dorminster Wilson. *Mother Scorpion Country*. San Francisco: Children's Book Press, 1987.

This picture book presents an important Miskito folktale about life, death, and love. The authors retell this haunting tale in both English and Spanish.

Rural Poverty in Honduras
http://www.ruralpovertyportal.org/web/guest/country/home/tags/honduras

This website explains the nature and effects of poverty in Honduras, with plenty of background info on the nation's geography, government, and economy to provide context. It also offers stories from real Hondurans living in poverty. Finally, it describes programs currently underway to help Hondurans lift themselves out of poverty.

vgsbooks.com
http://www.vgsbooks.com

Visit vgsbooks.com, the homepage of the Visual Geography Series®. You can get linked to all sorts of useful online information, including geographical, historical, demographic, cultural, and economic websites. The vgsbooks.com site is a great resource for late-breaking news and statistics.

Virtual Museum of Art of Honduras
http://www.honduras.com/museum/museo.html

Visitors to this website can view dozens of works by Honduran artists. The site includes precolonial, colonial, post-independence, and modern works.

Captions for photos appearing on cover and chapter openers:

Cover: Pico Bonito, a mountain in the Cordillera Nombre de Dios range, lies near the city of La Ceiba on the Caribbean coast of Honduras. Many people hike in Pico Bonito National Park.

pp. 4–5 Honduras has many beautiful beaches. This beach, on the northern coast of Roatán Island in the Caribbean Sea, is very popular with tourists.

pp. 8–9 Much of Honduras is mountainous. This isolated village is in the mountains near Yuscarán.

pp. 20–21 The ancient Maya ruins at Copán are a major tourist attraction. The city was a cultural center of the Maya civilization.

pp. 38–39 Honduras is home to many ethnic groups. Most Hondurans are of mixed racial heritage.

pp. 48–49 Many Hondurans are Catholic. They attend Mass in churches such as the San Pedro Cathedral in San Pedro Sula.

pp. 58–59 Bananas have been an important Honduran export for more than a century. Honduras has worked to diversify its exports and stabilize the economy.

Photo Acknowledgments

The images in this book are used with the permission of: © Ezra Millstein, pp. 4–5, 12, 15, 18, 20–21, 40 (both), 48–49, 56, 58–59, 65; © XNR Productions, pp. 6, 10; AP Photo/Gregory Bull, p. 7; © age fotostock/SuperStock, pp. 8–9; AP Photo/Ginnette Riquelme, p. 17; © Frederic Lewis/Hulton Archive/Getty Images, p. 23; © Stock Montage/Hulton Archive/Getty Images, p. 24 (top); © Scala/Art Resource, NY, p. 24 (bottom); The Art Archive/Simon Bolivar Amphitheatre Mexico/Gianni Dagli Orti, p. 27; AP Photo/HM, p. 34; © David Grossman/Alamy, p. 35; AP Photo/Julie Jacobson, p. 37; © Cory Langley, pp. 38–39, 45; © Giacomo Pirozzi/Panos Pictures, pp. 41, 43; © Paul Smith/Panos Pictures, p. 42; © Hemis.fr/SuperStock, p. 46; © Jeff Greenberg/Art Directors & TRIP, p. 50; © Orlando Sierra/AFP/Getty Images, p. 55; © Victor Englebert, p. 60; © Sean Sprague/Panos Pictures, p. 62; © Michele Burgess/SuperStock, p. 68; © Laura Westlund/Independent Picture Service, p. 69.

Front Cover: © M. Timothy O'Keefe/Alamy.